ACADEMIC
STUDIES
PRESS

Studies in Russian and Slavic
Literatures, Cultures and History

Series Editor: **Lazar Fleishman**

A "Labyrinth of Linkages"
In Tolstoy's *Anna Karenina*

Gary L. Browning

Academic Studies Press | 2010 |

Library of Congress Cataloging-in-Publication Data
Browning, Gary L.
 A "labyrinth of linkages" in Tolstoy's Anna Karenina / Gary L. Browning.
   p. cm. — (Studies in Russian and Slavic literatures, cultures and history)
 Includes bibliographical references and index.
 ISBN 978-1-936235-18-6 (hardback) — ISBN 978-1-936235-47-6 (pbk.) 1. Tolstoy, Leo, graf, 1828-1910. Anna Karenina. I. Title.
 PG3365.A63B76 2010
 891.73'3—dc22
                    2010024816

Book design by Ivan Grave

Published by Academic Studies Press in 2010
28 Montfern Avenue
Brighton, MA 02135, USA
press@academicstudiespress.com
www.academicstudiespress.com

For *Joan,*

Tom,

Don,

David

CONTENTS

Acknowledgements — 9

Author's note — 10

Introduction — 11

Chapter 1
Symbolism: The Train Ride — 24

Chapter 2
Symbolism: The Muzhik (Peasant) — 33

Chapter 3
Allegory: The Steeplechase Participants — 59

Chapter 4
Allegory: The Steeplechase's Recurring Motifs — 69

Chapter 5
Comparison of Early and Final Drafts Containing the Steeplechase Allegory and the Muzhik Symbol — 103

Conclusion — 115

Select Bibliography — 120

Index — 126

ACKNOWLEDGEMENTS

For generous professional development and financial support, I sincerely thank my Brigham Young University College of Humanities administrators, Department of Germanic and Slavic Languages and Literatures administrators and colleagues, and the Eliza R. Snow Fellowship committee. I deeply appreciate those who read my manuscript and made many perceptive comments, including Thomas F. Rogers, Caryl Emerson, Donna T. Orwin, David Sloane, David and LaRayne Hart, Debi Browning Dixon, and Lazar Fleishman. Additionally, several fine undergraduate research assistants contributed much, especially Rachel Wilcox, who assisted me over a considerable period of time.

I express appreciation to the editors of *Slavic and East European Journal* and *Russian Language Journal* for permission to publish revised and expanded versions of my articles which originally appeared in their journals:

"The Death of Anna Karenina: Anna's Share of the Blame," SEEJ, vol. 20, no. 3 (Fall 1986):327-39.

"Peasant Dreams in *Anna Karenina*," SEEJ, vol. 44, no. 4 (Winter 2000):525-36.

"Steeplechase Themes in *Anna Karenina*," RLJ, xliii, nos. 145-46 (1989):113-30.

AUTHOR'S NOTE

In addition to utilizing English quotations from the excellent 2001 Richard Pevear and Larissa Volokhonsky translation of *Anna Karenina*, on occasion I also provide the Russian original. Generally, for English speakers the English translation will be entirely adequate. However, for those fluent both in English and Russian, the Russian original will highlight and clarify nuances between the languages. Infrequently, I have considered the translation to be imprecise or even incorrect, as shown in the text below.

INTRODUCTION

Among the difficult challenges facing a literary scholar is that of resisting the inclination to over-interpret; that is, to impose a burden of extraneous insight upon a text. Like many before me, I agree that a critic's perceptions should arise from and find adequate support in the literary text. In this study, that text is Leo Tolstoy's *Anna Karenina* (1878), about which Edward Wasiolek famously remarked:

> In reading *Anna Karenina* we are in the presence of one of those great texts, the structure of which is multiple and which in its richness can support a great number — perhaps an inexhaustible number — of explanations. (Wasiolek 155)

Nevertheless, in literary scholarship an interpretation or analysis should be grounded in the *text*, not displace or obfuscate it.

In this study, I will focus on the fictional characters for whom Tolstoy provides, in addition to their dominant realistic portrayals, layers of symbol and allegory. My main emphasis will be on Anna Karenina and Alexei Vronsky, and to a lesser extent on Alexei and Seryozha Karenin. My underlying mode of inquiry will be *moral criticism* as facilitated through tools of *rhetorical* and *structural criticism*. I seek to demonstrate that Tolstoy's fundamental moral message is not merely direct and open, but also subtly embedded in symbol and allegory, and reinforced by an intricate and sophisticated formal structure.

Tolstoy is renowned as a leading proponent of Russian *realistic* prose fiction. One expects his writing to help define and exemplify important features of that genre, such as precision of observation, verisimilitude, contemporary settings, and a preference for metonymy — a significant metaphorical image revealing essential meaning through related attributes or associations. By these and similar standards *Anna Karenina* is, indeed, an impressive realistic novel. However, at the height of his creative powers and in what is generally considered preeminent among his finest realistic works, Tolstoy includes significant elements of symbol[1] and allegory.

In *Anna Karenina*, Tolstoy's artistic inclinations differ from both his previous and his later use of more realistic, metonymic imagery, such as that found in *War and Peace*'s budding oak tree, which Prince Andrey Bolkonsky encounters on his way to and from the Rostov estate, or in *Hadji Murat*'s rugged thistle, described at the beginning and end of the novella. These images are rich and memorable metonyms. The bare, then fully leafed-out oak tree in *War and Peace* suggests the renewal of Andrey's emotional vitality and resurgent feelings of love. The crushed but resilient thistle in *Hadji Murat* corresponds to Hadji's indomitable spirit. In each case the image is artistically impressive, but relatively direct and immediately accessible in its meaning, not ineffably symbolic or intricately allegorical.

Tolstoy overlays *Anna Karenina*'s realism with symbol and allegory to a degree entirely unknown in the author's

---

[1] Other terms applied to the symbolic facets of *Anna Karenina* include proto-symbolism, quasi-symbolism, pre-symbolism, emblematic realism (Gustafson 202-13), and iconic aesthetics (Mandelker 58-80). For helpful treatments of this topic, see the informative *Tolstoy Studies Journal* special issue on *Anna Karenina* (VIII, 1995-96). Several of its articles refer to aspects of symbolism in *Anna Karenina*, especially articles by Liza Knapp, Justin Weir, and James Rice, as well as important contributions by Caryl Emerson and Donna Orwin in the issue's Roundtable Discussion.

other works. The leading early Russian Tolstoy scholar Boris Eikhenbaum, along with others after him, attributes much of the novel's symbolic impulse to the German philosopher Arthur Schopenhauer and the Russian poets Afanasii Fet and, especially, Fedor Tiutchev (189-91). Tolstoy read and admired all three of these writers at the time he was preparing to write *Anna Karenina.* However, it is not my purpose here to seek or evaluate literary influences, but to analyze in a more focused manner Tolstoy's impressive utilization of symbol, allegory, and structural patterning in support of his principal moral views in *Anna Karenina.*

To formulate a working definition of the terms allegory and symbol, I refer first to Simon Brittan's helpful treatment, in which he quotes from Goethe:

> *Allegory* transforms experience into a *concept* and a concept into an *image,* but so that the concept remains always defined and expressible by the image; a *symbol* transforms experience into an *idea* and an idea into an *image,* so that the idea expressed through the image remains always active and unattainable. (170-71; emphasis added)

To illustrate, in an allegory the concept [such as Anna Karenina's attitude of willing sacrifice for Vronsky] and its image [the steeplechase horse Frou-Frou's immediate response to her rider's wish] remain "defined and expressible by the image."

In a symbol the idea [for example, debased human love] and its image [a repulsive, French-speaking Russian muzhik (peasant)] remain "active and unattainable." In the more transparent mode of allegory, image and meaning have a closer, nearly one-to-one relationship, whereas symbols are much less precisely expressible and more actively encompass additional facets of meaning.

For purposes of this study, an additional perspective should be included: "Symbol is distinguished from allegory in that the allegorical figure has no meaning apart from the idea it is meant to indicate within the structure of the allegory, whereas a symbol has a meaning independent of the rest of the narrative in which it appears" (*Encyclopedia of Literature* 1085). This perspective is a key to understanding Tolstoy's use of allegory and symbol. For instance, apart from Anna, the horse Frou-Frou has no meaning beyond the steeplechase, while the French-speaking muzhik is a peculiar, chilling manifestation of a deep, pervasive, and more universal meaning loosely associated, in part, with selfish, debased emotion.

Finally, while readers may feel relatively confident they have understood an allegory, William York Tindall cautions them against claiming to have fully apprehended a symbol:

> The trouble with the symbol as communicator is that, although definite in being the semblance of an articulated object, it is indefinite in what it presents. In the first place the symbol is an analogy for something undefined and in the second our apprehension of the analogy is commonly incomplete. Moreover, the terms of the analogy are confused. (16)

As discussed in greater detail in chapter three, the novel's named participants in the *steeplechase* are allegorical in significant ways. Frou-Frou partially represents Anna Karenina, as, to a considerable degree, do the horse Gladiator and his rider Makhotin represent Karenin and his and Anna's son, Seryozha. In Tolstoy's terms, the whole steeplechase is an extended, elaborate, and quite complex allegory. The allegory relates to an amalgamation of stresses and barriers arising from abandonment of family and a futile search (race) for greater happiness in an extra-marital relationship. On the other hand, as will be shown in detail in chapter two, Anna is pursued by a specter that is considerably more symbolic than allegorical — the disheveled, repulsive muzhik of Anna's recurring nightmares.

In *Anna Karenina* a cluster of *symbolic images* forms around Anna's train ride from Moscow back to St. Petersburg after Anna has smoothed over the Oblonsky marital discord. Regarding aspects which combine to constitute the symbolic dimension of the *train* itself, at least three principal levels are discernable. The first is the *realistic* level, the level *outside* of the author, observable and understandable in everyday life. Thus, the train in *Anna Karenina* is a means of convenient and swift conveyance. The second level is *metaphysical* and *above* the author, or beyond and transcending the realistic level. Here the train may further suggest the means through which one passes across traditional boundaries and moral restraints, a looming danger, and an instrument of harm or even death. The third level is *personal* or *within* and characteristic of the author. It emanates from the author's own experience, perceptions, and preferences or biases. On this level the train may find affiliation with forces that enable immoral behavior and, in a related sphere, facilitate random, unrestrained movement, the growth of cities and factories, and the undermining of a traditional, comparatively wholesome agricultural economy (484).

Much of the profound imagery in *Anna Karenina* includes features both of allegory and symbol, and constitutes a conspicuous departure from the author's method before and after *Anna Karenina*. For instance, in his post-*Anna Karenina* period, on occasion Tolstoy uses forms of allegory, especially the parable, in moralistic writings such as in "How Much Land Does a Man Need?" or "The Three Hermits," both published in 1886. In these and other works, his allegory is essentially devoid of symbolic aspiration or pretension.

One additional methodological tool requires comment. In reading *Anna Karenina* for moral insight through symbolic and allegorical tropes and/or through structural patterning, I have employed a form of inductive reasoning that may be called the *principle of reasonable probability*. Utilizing this principle, I have discovered several inadequately analyzed manifestations of symbol, allegory, and structural patterning in the text. For example, since the steeplechase's allegorical parallels between Frou-Frou and Anna are relatively apparent and widely acknowledged, I have invoked the *principle of reasonable probability* to explore the possibility of allegorically interpreting other *named* horses and their riders. This in turn led me to discover the aforementioned and hereafter discussed associations between the horse Gladiator and Karenin, and between the rider Makhotin and Seryozha.

Such parallels yield allegorical implications, but also on occasion open the door to further possibilities for symbolic interpretation. Again, I consider it essential to refrain from confident assertions without sufficient grounding in the text. Still, utilizing the *principle of reasonable probability*, one may more readily recognize quite solid if occasionally sparse textual support for additional connections or linkages. In a rather different, scientifically more precise way, something akin to the *principle of reasonable probability* has led astronomers to predict the exact location of as yet undiscovered planets, chemists to fill out the Periodic Table with previously unidentified elements, and linguists to reconstruct ancient languages.

As applied to literature, the *principle of reasonable probability* suggests that in a given text where one observes a significant technique, idea, or device, additional similar forms and expressions are more likely to emerge as intentional, not merely random or coincidental occurrences. There is no certainty they will occur, but the *principle of reasonable probability* stimulates additional investigation and, at times, discovery. A final illustration of this point: a single instance of a full-fledged symbol, such as the repulsive muzhik in *Anna Karenina*, encourages one to ask whether other images might have a similarly symbolic inclination and function. That heightened awareness then leads to an expectation of symbolic meaning such as those found in a storm, the cold post (hand railing), loose sheet of iron, train wheels and rails, and the penknife, among others, all discussed below.

Before writing *Anna Karenina*, Tolstoy already had used allegory in his work, as in his early short story "Three Deaths" (1859). But what of symbolic elements? Do we know whether the author *intended* to include symbolic features in *Anna Karenina*? While following the trail of several apparent symbolic images in *Anna Karenina*, I wondered whether Tolstoy ever spoke or wrote about an *intention* to experiment with symbolic images in this great novel. I have found little of weighty substance, with the exception of two tantalizing and often-quoted, but ever intriguing, excerpts from Tolstoy's letters.

The first quotation calls upon the literary scholar to direct close attention to *linkages* [*сцепления*] in *Anna Karenina*. This challenge, contained in a letter of 23 April, 1876, written as Tolstoy nears completion of *Anna Karenina*, is addressed to his friend and critic, the philosopher Nikolai Strakhov.

In the letter, Tolstoy upbraids readers who are drawn primarily or even solely to realistic details in *Anna Karenina*. He invites the critic to search for its more subtle ideas, which are *linked together* to form essential, composite, complex meanings. These linkages, as is characteristic of symbols, cannot be fathomed by an analysis of individual parts, but only through interwoven and mutually enhancing strands of meaning. Like a tapestry whose patterns and beauty appear only as many complementary and contrasting threads are woven together, significant meaning within *Anna Karenina* emerges through linkages or connections of discreet but resonant ideas. Quoting from Tolstoy's letter to Strakhov about *Anna Karenina*:

> If myopic critics think I only wanted to describe what attracts my attention — how Oblonsky dines or what kind of shoulders Anna has — they miss the point. In almost everything I wrote I was driven by the need to combine *ideas linked together for their expression. But each idea expressed separately loses its meaning, and becomes terribly degraded if apart from that linkage to which it belongs.* I think the linkage itself is composed not of an idea, but of something else. *It is impossible to express the essence of a linkage directly in words.* It is only possible indirectly — through words describing images, actions and situations. . . . What literary criticism needs are those who would show the foolishness of searching merely for a literary work's ideas. *Critics should continually lead readers through the endless labyrinth of linkages forming the essence of art to those laws serving as the basis for these linkages.* (Tolstoy, *Polnoe sobranie* 62:268-69; emphasis added)

In my view, a "labyrinth of linkages" decidedly underlies the richness of both symbol and allegory in *Anna Karenina*. Certain linkages, for instance those from the steeplechase, do recur and develop in other parts of the novel. One example arises at the end of the steeplechase. Vronsky's "failure to keep pace" (Blackmur 907) with Frou-Frou, his standing up in the saddle, then sitting down at precisely the wrong moment as Frou-Frou apparently leaps upward, directly results in Frou-Frou's death. As will be shown below, while Frou-Frou dies once, Anna "dies" four times in the novel, finally, in the last instance, literally. These four deaths form linkages that underscore an allegorical meaning connected with the broad theme of *violation* and *reckoning*, as implied by the novel's very epigraph, "vengeance is mine; I will repay" (Romans 12:19).

A second relevant quotation occurs in Tolstoy's letter written nine months later on 27 January 1877 to another friend, S.A. Rachinskii. Speaking of *Anna Karenina*, Tolstoy virtually taunts his readers to try to discover the "keystone" to its "architecture" or structure. That keystone, the author again insists, resides in its internal unities, rather than in the story line or character relationships. As Tolstoy writes:

> I am proud . . . of the [novel's] architecture — the arches are joined so that *it is impossible to distinguish the keystone* [замок]. *And I strove for that result above all.* The structural unity [связь] arises not from the story, nor from characters' relationships (their acquaintance), but from an *internal unity.* . . . I fear that, having sped through the novel, you have missed its *inner unity.* . . . *That which I understand as the unity is what has made this whole thing significant for me. The unity is there — look carefully and you will find it.* (Tolstoy, *Polnoe sobranie* 62:377; emphasis added)

I propose that two principal linkages or unities explored hereafter form keystones which emerge, first, during Anna's train ride from Moscow to St. Petersburg and, second, in Vronsky's steeplechase (horse race).

While the foregoing quotations from letters to Strakhov and Rachinskii conceivably apply to allegory and symbol, they may relate to other aspects of Tolstoy's writing as well. Thus, we readers are left without conclusive external evidence of the author's intentions or of *Anna Karenina*'s indisputable meaning. It is as though for personal reasons Tolstoy the realist and putative opponent of emphasis on technique or form has chosen not to reveal more concerning his subjective purposes in employing allegory, symbol, and structural patterning. Perhaps at some deeper level and with a degree of unsettled conscience, he senses that not only is Anna guilty of infidelity, but so too is her creator, ostensibly a master solely of Russian realistic prose. However, as always, what is finally most important is the completed text itself. It is within the novel's text, not extraneous sources, that we must search for clues to any "linkages," "unities," and "keystones." If they exist, they will be found in the text, requiring the reader to discern the meaning, significance, and prominence of such clues.

Many would agree that certain symbolic images in *Anna Karenina* are inadequately developed and quite superficial. Recall, for example, Anna's red handbag as seen near the beginning and again at the end of Anna's appearances in the novel. Generally, what has been written about the handbag, some of it quite detailed and imaginative, is tenuously connected to the text, and, in my opinion, often rather too reliant on Freudian implications.[2] Still, it does appear to many readers that the handbag can be associated with Anna's passion for a full, robust life, including, more centrally important, a fulfilling physical love.[3] But in the novel, the red handbag image appears sparsely and is meagerly developed. The critic may be well advised to refrain from *over*-analyzing such relatively insignificant symbolic images.

Certain other symbols are highly conventional and quite unremarkable, such as the universal and overworked symbol of a burning candle, seen both in *War and Peace* as Lise Bolkonskaya lies dying and several times in *Anna Karenina*, especially as Anna contemplates or actually experiences

---

[2] For example, see Thomas Barran (161-65). For more detailed, persuasive, and less Freudian treatments see Barbara Lönnquist (80-89), and Liza Knapp (91-93).

[3] See especially Richard Gustafson (309-13) for his thoughtful discussion of the red handbag as Anna's bag of desires and pleasures.

death. This tired symbol too obviously suggests the passage of time throughout a person's life. Finally the candles, Lise, and Anna expire. Little can be said of substance, though a considerable amount has been written[4] about this standard, frail symbol, except to recognize that in general it is, though modestly significant, readily apparent and clichéd.

By contrast, two developing and multi-faceted *clusters* of symbols and allegories play larger, broadly illuminating roles in the novel. An awareness of these two principal clusters significantly contributes to a fuller understanding and appreciation of Tolstoy's remarkably rich novel.

The *first such cluster of symbols* begins to form early in the novel from several images connected with Anna's evocative, finally hallucinatory train ride from Moscow back to St. Petersburg after she has reconciled Dolly to Stiva Oblonsky. Most important, the shadow of a stooping man apparently striking train wheels with a hammer to test their soundness will gradually develop, deepen, and find association with the muzhik in Anna's nightmares. This muzhik, in part, will embody her revulsion toward soulless, degrading, perverse love. Finally the image will emerge as a full-fledged symbol, including an embedded allegorical substratum — the muzhik at one level also represents both Karenin and Vronsky. The *second cluster is more allegorical* rather than symbolic, and arises from the steeplechase episode, at the end of which Vronsky breaks Frou-Frou's back. Much more will be said about both clusters hereafter.

A potential *third cluster* dissipates before it has fully formed. This minor allegorical cluster involves Levin's early ice-skating encounter with Kitty. Levin's agility, strength,

---

[4] For example, see Bilinkis (70-71). On the other hand, with his elegant system of "hermeneutic indices," Vladimir Alexandrov reveals previously uncommented-upon possibilities for interpreting the candle beyond the traditional function suggesting "passage of time" (80-83).

and courage are evident as he attempts a new and difficult skating maneuver, nearly trips, but adroitly recovers his balance and skates on triumphantly. This image foreshadows and encapsulates his ultimately successful relations with Kitty, but is slight and undeveloped. It remains only weakly connected or linked to the remainder of the novel. Levin does falter after Kitty's refusal of his first proposal of marriage, then, after a rather too long period of wounded pride and withdrawal, regains his footing and refocuses his hopes on Kitty. But this is not nearly a weighty enough cluster to require treatment here. In the novel, Levin, Tolstoy's surrogate, remains distinctly realistic, without sustained allegorical or symbolic dimensions. Allegory and symbol emerge readily from Anna and Vronsky, whose lives are more "literary," as contrasted to the more "autobiographical" Levin.

The two more fully developed clusters, one largely of symbols and the other of allegories, are deeply significant. It is here, for instance, that the reader learns of Anna and Vronsky's principal personal weaknesses, in contrast to their abundant appealing features. However, it is their flaws that will lead to a gradual dissolution of their relationship, to Anna's suicide, and to Vronsky's debilitating despair. These weaknesses may be summarized graphically as follows:

Vronsky's "failure to keep pace" seen in his:
- awkward movements (responses) at critical moments;
- insensitivity and obtuseness in relation to Anna's deepest needs;
- and excessive self-absorption and pride.

Anna's failure to remain grounded in reality seen in her:
- yielding to romantic fantasy and self-indulgence;
- reluctance to recognize or accept responsibility and, especially, blame;
- willing escape into a second, baser personality;

- and recourse to deception and delusion of self and others.[5]

In the following chapters, I will identify the main components of the two primary clusters of symbolic and allegorical images from the train ride and steeplechase as portrayed in the final text of *Anna Karenina*,[6] analyze the meanings and significance of these components, and sketch the development of these key symbolic and allegorical elements through the two earliest drafts of the novel. Further, I will reveal how the novel's structure or "architecture" contributes greatly but subtly to an elaboration of Tolstoy's emphatic moral message.

---

[5] Anna's weaknesses are seen, for example, as she first settles into her train seat. She assures herself that she is relieved to be leaving Moscow and Vronsky. But soon, from barely under the surface, another, baser side of Anna emerges. As she falls under the sway of her romantic English novel and recalls Vronsky at the ball [yielding to romantic fantasy], Anna tries to convince herself "nothing was shameful" (100) [reluctance to recognize or accept responsibility and blame], although an inner voice causes her to feel culpable. Soon Anna's fertile imagination engages and she drifts into a state of near-delirium, leading her to question whether she is "myself or someone else" [willing escape into a second, baser personality]. While it was frightening to surrender herself to this oblivion, something was drawing her in, and she was able, at will, to surrender to it or hold back from it" (101; emphasis added) [recourse to deception and delusion of self and others].

[6] All English quotations are from the recent and more accurate Richard Pevear and Larissa Volokhonsky translation of *Anna Karenina*: New York: Viking Press, 2001. Unless otherwise noted, Russian quotations are from Tolstoy's relatively widely available and textually more reliable Tolstoy, L.N., *Sobranie sochinenii v dvadtsati tomakh*, red. N.N. Akopova, Moskva: Gosizdat "Khudozhestvennaia literatura," 1960-65, tt. 8-9, 1963.

Chapter 1

SYMBOLISM:
THE TRAIN RIDE

Having effected a reconciliation of the Moscow Oblonskys, Anna returns by train to her family in St. Petersburg. During this ride, several minor symbolic images emerge. While Anna's aforementioned *red handbag* and the small *pillow* and *English novel* she takes from it are embryos of symbolic impulse, their roles essentially are decorative and, finally, relatively insignificant. Furthermore, the universal *candle* symbol makes its first of several appearances here in the reading lantern attached to Anna's train seat, but it is so common and predictable a literary device that it contributes little to the novel's meaning.

Two potentially more important symbols connected to the train ride merit comment. A *storm* rages at the Bologovo station, significantly located midway between St. Petersburg and Moscow — paralleling Anna's emotions and memories attached both to her family in St. Petersburg and, more recently, to Vronsky in Moscow. As Anna told Dolly, "I was so reluctant to leave Petersburg, and now — to leave here" (97). This storm symbol begins very impressively, but loses its force and prominence as the novel progresses. Similarly, the *cold post* (hand rail) image of stolid uprightness appears primarily in this one small but momentous Bologovo station episode. The post has the potential of becoming a modestly significant symbol, but owing to its arrested development, remains little more than an impressive metonymic detail.

However, if one were to consider only the train ride episode, there is little doubt that the most meaningful tropes would relate to the *storm* and *cold post* symbolic images. From the time of the train ride back to St. Petersburg until Anna's death, nothing so fully reveals the darker essence of Anna's mounting emotional and moral vulnerability than the storm. With its violent, destructive outbursts interspersed with periods of relative calm, the storm encapsulates Anna's approaching relationship with Vronsky. The storm is memorably introduced first in "the semi-darkness of the sleeping car" (99). Here the temperature changes in "quick transitions from steaming heat to cold and back to heat" (100), foreshadowing Anna's volatile feelings for Vronsky now and subsequently. These relations pass inexorably through emotional storms of increasing intensity, mounting to a destructive force at the time of the heroine's violent death, again set in the context of train imagery.

Recalling the railroad workman's portentous death as Anna arrived in Moscow a few days earlier[1] and foretelling Anna's subsequent death, also under the wheels of a train car, Anna on her way back to St. Petersburg perceives that "something screeched and banged terribly, as if someone was being torn to pieces." Immediately following, "a red fire blinded her eyes, and then everything was hidden by a wall [death]. . . . But all this was not frightening but exhilarating" (101).

At the Bologovo station Anna steps onto the platform and into a "terrible snowstorm," now revealing a third dimension of the storm's function. Not only does the storm connect Anna to her troubling relations with Vronsky and to her own eventual death, but also to her unstable emotional

---

[1] R.L. Jackson (Chance 315-29) carefully analyzes Tolstoy's skillful foreshadowing through motifs surrounding Anna's arrival in Moscow, meeting Vronsky, and learning of the peasant run over by a train.

landscape. The storm "would subside for a moment, but then return again in such gusts that it seemed impossible to withstand it" (102). Upon Anna's experience of irrepressible delight as she sees Vronsky on the platform and hears him declare he is traveling "in order to be where you are," the full force of the powerful storm and train erupts in foreboding: "as if overcoming an obstacle, the wind dumped snow from the roof of the carriage, blew a *torn-off sheet of iron* about, and from ahead a low train whistle howled mournfully and drearily" (103; emphasis added). Anna's explosive passion now and periodically henceforth will evoke the storm's frenzy of elemental wildness, a careening mortal threat and a gloomy signal of approaching sorrow.

At this early juncture, significantly, Anna has the power either to refrain from or yield to the storm within and about, but this capacity to refrain gradually diminishes, until it finally disappears at the time of her death. Recall an event on the day before Anna's suicide when somehow she is able to recover momentarily as Yashvin's entry into her apartment interrupts a particularly nasty argument with Vronsky: "Having instantly calmed the *storm* within her, she sat down and began talking with the visitor" (749; emphasis added). But this is only a brief calm, followed within a day by the final uncontrollable tempest culminating in Anna's suicide.

Also at the Bologovo station, another briefly important incipient symbol appears in contrast to the calamitous, impassioned storm. Four times Anna attempts to steady herself by reaching for a cold *post* (*stolb*) or handrail at the steps to her train car. The post itself suggests several intersecting dimensions of uprightness, including moral stability, societal propriety and marital fidelity. Figuratively, Anna eventually loosens her grip on the post and slips toward self-indulgence.

To review the four instances: first, as Anna descends the steps from the train, "the wind, as if only waiting for her, whistled joyfully and wanted to pick her up and carry her off, but she grasped the *cold post* firmly and, holding her dress down, stepped onto the platform" (101; emphasis added). Then, having inhaled the refreshing, snowy air, she "had already taken her hand from her muff to grasp the *post* and go back into the carriage" (102), when she encounters Vronsky. Next, sensing why Vronsky is traveling on her same train, she addresses him, "letting fall the hand that was already holding the *post*" (103). Following their brief but intense conversation, Anna reluctantly climbs the steps back into her train car, "placing her hand on the *cold post*," while sensing "this momentary conversation had brought them terribly close, and this made her both frightened and happy. . . . She did not sleep all night" (103). Contrasting starkly to the cold post of probity are Anna's nighttime reveries, in which "there was nothing unpleasant or gloomy; on the contrary, there was something joyful, burning, and exciting" (103) [or *arousing, возбуждающее*].

In a perceptive article on the image of the railroad in *Anna Karenina*, Gary Jahn portrays the railroad as a

> representation of the requirements and privileges of the social in the context of the thematic exploration of the conflict between the desires of the individual and the restrictions placed upon the gratification of those desires by the social. (8)

I further propose that the *cold post* appears as an embryonic symbol, but remains a substantial metonymy, associated with the more symbolic railroad, that is, a rather concrete metonym for the "requirements and privileges of the social" — society's firm, unyielding, iron-clad norms imposed upon an individual despite her yearning for liberation. As Jahn explains, Anna

Symbolism: The Train Ride

is torn between the societal demands of a Charybdis and a Scylla striving for "unrestrained gratification" (8).

Finally, in *Anna Karenina* another moderately developed symbolic image initially affiliated with the train ride sequence forms a second contrasting pair with the cold post. This symbol is the *knife*. If the cold post relates to a moral resolve which society hypocritically expounds, but does not embody, the knife is more closely associated with severance of restraints, the "cutting of bonds" (Jackson, "Night Journey," 153). To review, Anna boards the train for St. Petersburg and "took a *paper-knife* and an English novel from her handbag" (99-100; emphasis added). The paper-knife, used at the time to cut apart pages of a new book, here functions as the key to a Pandora's box of fantasy. It will be mentioned three more times in quick succession and then, on occasion, subsequently throughout the novel. Gradually the knife acquires a fuller, although still quite modest, symbolic character.

The book's pages now cut open, Anna reads of a woman heroically sacrificing herself in order to care for a man who is ill, a member of Parliament delivering a speech, and a bold lady hunting with hounds — all engaged in out-of-the-ordinary, demanding but fulfilling tasks. Anna yearns to be involved in similar activities herself, not merely to read passively about them. "But there was nothing to do, and so, fingering the *smooth knife* with her small hands, she forced herself to read" (100). The knife is at the ready to cut asunder dull, benumbing restraints and to liberate new, enlivening possibilities.

Moments later, her imagination freed, Anna wishes she could accompany the novel's hero to his country estate, but feels ashamed of this desire. Rationalizing these feelings of guilt, she "put down the book and leaned back in the seat, clutching the *paper-knife* tightly in both hands" (100), possibly preparing to defend herself from further hindrances to her enjoyment. Presently Anna gives full reign to her sensual imagination:

> She passed the paper-knife over the glass, then put its smooth and cold surface to her cheek and nearly laughed aloud from the joy that suddenly came over her for no reason. She felt her nerves tighten more and more, like strings on winding pegs. She felt her eyes open wider and wider, her fingers and toes move nervously; something inside her stopped her breath, and all images and sounds in that wavering semi-darkness impressed themselves on her with extraordinary vividness. She kept having moments of doubt whether the carriage was moving forward or backwards, or standing still.[2] (101; emphasis added)

In this setting and in others to follow, the smooth, cold knife acquires symbolic stature. Considering the whole array of knife references in the novel, one may view the knife as an instrument of power and aggression, capable of severing from its possessor former restraints and relationships, and carving space for new impulses and expressions of the liberated self, thus contrasting with the cold post of societal propriety, decorum, and temperance.

In a subsequent occurrence, the paper-knife is in Karenin's hands. As he awaits Anna's return from Betsy's soirée, at which Anna and Vronsky sit apart from all others while conversing at length, and after which Vronsky feels he has made great progress in his quest for Anna's heart, Karenin "opened a book about the papacy at a place marked by a *paper-knife*, and read till one o'clock." (142). The significance of this ostensibly random detail becomes clearer later in the novel

---

[2] Its levels and possibilities for interpretation are many, including, as in the foregoing passage, sexual. Cf. Edward Wasiolek: "The knife may be taken as a detail signifying the destructive possibility of the passion, especially in a context that is manifestly sexual" (135).

Symbolism: The Train Ride

as Karenin reads his just-completed note to Anna following her confession to him that she is Vronsky's mistress. In the note, Karenin states his expectations for her future behavior and summons her back to Petersburg. Then, "having folded the letter, smoothed it with a massive ivory *paper-knife*, and put money in the envelope," Karen orders tea and begins "toying with the massive *paper-knife*" before reading further in his book (284). Here the knife again seems associated with his power to sever old commitments and to shape and impose a new order on his relationship with Anna.

The knife also appears in less significant contexts, for instance when Dolly pleads Anna's case to Karenin in her Moscow home, where Anna much earlier had reconciled Dolly to her husband. Karenin "got up and obediently followed her to the schoolroom. They sat down at a table covered with oilcloth cut all over by *penknives*" (393), reflecting the activity of Dolly's children and possibly suggesting an inclination toward cutting away childhood restraints and establishing greater independence. Then, near the time Anna visits her son on his birthday, Seryozha, awaiting his father's arrival, "sat at the desk playing with his *penknife*" (523) and begins to consider his mother. Subconsciously Seryozha may be thinking about severing the fetters that now prevent him, as he imagines, from returning to his mother's more compassionate care.

Next, after her visit to Seryozha, Anna feels desolate and helpless while viewing photographs of her son: "As there was no *paper-knife* on the table, she took out the picture next to it (it was a picture of Vronsky in a round hat and with long hair, taken in Rome) and pushed her son's picture out with it" (539). In this instance, Vronsky's photograph functions in Anna's hands as a surrogate knife, responsible, as is Vronsky, for severing a cherished relationship she longs to recover.

The final paper-knife image appears as Levin visits Kitty's levelheaded sister Natalie and her diplomat husband Lvov. While discussing parent-child relations as Kitty prepares to give birth, Natalie opines that extreme child-raising theories should be avoided. Natalie then applies this principle to life in general: "'No, extremes aren't good in anything,' Natalie said calmly, putting his *paper-knife* in its proper place on the desk" (684). As though stripping the knife of its symbolic valences of power, dominance, compulsion, and severance from prevailing status, she unceremoniously relegates the knife to its accustomed place and the anticipated, limited, realistic role it normally plays.

The incipient symbolic imagery introduced through the train ride, including the gusting storm; the wind-blown, torn-off sheet of iron; the cold post; and the knife, are engaging, but at last, too slight to sustain extended analysis or to attain full status as symbols. However, the sheet of iron, discussed further in chapter two below, will find a significant role in the most complex symbol in all of Tolstoy's writing — the perplexing and chilling Russian muzhik of Vronsky's and especially Anna's nightmares.

Chapter 2

SYMBOLISM:
THE MUZHIK (PEASANT)

By far the most robust and significant symbol recurs at intervals throughout the novel and, again, first appears during Anna's train ride home from Moscow to St. Petersburg as she stops at the Bologovo station.[1] This symbol revolves around a muzhik, here referred to simply as a "huddled shadow of a man." This shadow "slipped under [Anna's] feet, and there was the noise of a hammer striking iron" (102). On the realistic level, apparently he is a railway employee merely verifying the soundness of the train's steel wheels. But as an emerging symbol, the shadow, especially as seen in Anna's subsequently recurring nightmares, will embody for her something much more consequential: a frightening image of vile, repulsive, dehumanized love, seen first in Karenin and, later, in Vronsky, both of whom Anna perceives as having become self-absorbed, indifferent, emotionally bereft lovers.

Two respected literary scholars previously suggested the interpretation I will extend and deepen. Richard Gustafson treats the evolution of the peasant dreams, initially, as an emblem of Vronsky and Anna's conscience "reacting in panic to her pregnancy," and then, as Vronsky alone, who

---

[1] Immediately before Anna arrives at the Bologovo station, she sees a "skinny muzhik" stove stoker examining the thermometer in her train car. Anna drifts again into her delusional state and perceives him as being more like a beast "gnawing something on the wall" (101). Some commentators see this image as being part of the novel's later muzhik symbol. However, I feel the skinny muzhik functions as a significant early indication of Anna's penchant for mentally transforming reality into fantasy or grotesquery.

Symbolism: The Muzhik (Peasant)

has "grown cold to her, paying no attention to her but doing something to her" in the final dream (Gustafson 311). Edward Wasiolek further observes that "the peasant who appears at this point [immediately following Anna's suicide] and who has appeared in her dreams is probably a symbol of the remorseless, impersonal power of sex. As he beats the iron, he pays no attention to her" (Wasiolek 153). Both of these literary critics allude to a connection between the peasant and debased physical intimacy.

I intend to substantiate and expand upon Gustafson and Wasiolek's readings, and to provide additional critical perspective on this centrally important symbol in *Anna Karenina*. From the text I will marshal evidence to demonstrate how the peasant *allegorically* represents a degraded Karenin and, then, Vronsky, and on the *symbolic level*, a more universal, metaphysical desecration and perversion of human love. In Karenin and Vronsky's case, degeneration occurs largely from Anna's unfortunate tendency to initially idealize and then, as inevitable disillusionment follows, despise her men. Since over time both Karenin and Vronsky prove incapable of entirely fulfilling her extravagant expectations, Anna subconsciously, gradually but ineluctably, transforms them mentally and emotionally into ignoble creatures, whose imagined appearance and conduct become those of a crude muzhik. Anna's eventual loss of all hope of obtaining her romantic ideal and the accompanying despair she feels at perceived insincere, insensitive, and emotionally insipid marital relations play a decisive role in driving her ultimately to self-destruction.

Considering Tolstoy's entire prose oeuvre, the small, dirty, hunched-over, French-speaking muzhik is certainly his most multifaceted, intriguing, and sophisticated symbol, both requiring and rewarding careful examination. To begin, in *Anna Karenina* at least nine principal occurrences are noteworthy, to a lesser or greater degree, in relation to this symbol:

1. Early in the novel, Vronsky goes to the Moscow train station to meet his mother, whose train from St. Petersburg has just arrived. He notices passengers getting off the train, among them "a muzhik with a sack over his shoulder" (60; *мужик с мешком через плечо* [8.76]).

2. While still at the train station, Vronsky and Anna learn that a watchman, "either drunk or too bundled up because of the freezing cold, had not heard a train being shunted and had been run over" (64). Vronsky sees the workman's "mangled corpse," and Anna feels the event to be a "bad omen" (65; *дурное предзнаменование* [8.81]).

3. Several days later, after reconciling the Moscow Oblonskys, Anna travels back to St. Petersburg. Her train stops at the Bologovo station and she detrains for a breath of fresh air. While on the platform, "the huddled shadow [*согнутая тень*: stooping or crouching shadow (8.124)] of a man slipped under her feet, and there was the noise of a hammer striking iron" (102).

4. Seconds later, Anna joyfully encounters Vronsky. He assures Anna he is traveling in order to be near her. Simultaneously the wind "blew some torn-off *sheet of iron* about" (103; emphasis added [*ветер . . . затрепал каким-то железным оторванным листом* {8.125}]).

5. Over a year-and-a-half later, Vronsky has a dream which, he soon learns, parallels that of Anna's. Vronsky's dream is quite sketchy and uncomplicated: "The muzhik tracker, I think, small, dirty, with a disheveled beard, was bending down [*нагнувшись* (8.417)] and doing something, and he suddenly said some strange words in French. Yes, that's all there was to the dream" (355). For reasons not yet evident, Vronsky awakens from this dream "trembling with fear."

Symbolism: The Muzhik (Peasant)

6. That same evening, Anna tells Vronsky of a terrifying nightmare she *recalls* from "long ago" (361). Anna's nightmare is more detailed and precise than Vronsky's, and takes place in her bedroom, into which she has run "to get something there, to find something out." She is startled to see a muzhik standing in the corner, "with a disheveled beard, small and frightening. I wanted to run away, but he bent over a sack [*нагнулся над мешком* (8.424)] and rummaged [*копошится*] in it with his hands." Anna "showed how he rummaged in the sack. There was horror in her face." Anna concludes her account: "He rummages and mutters [*приговаривает*: keeps repeating, chanting] in French, very quickly, and rolling the *r*s in his throat, you know: *Il faut le battre le fer, le broyer, le pétrir*," translated as, "You must beat the iron, pound it, knead it" (361).

7. On the morning of Anna's suicide, approximately two years after telling Vronsky of her frightening dream, she again experiences the muzhik nightmare.[2] Now Anna provides this especially significant restatement of her recurring dream:

> A little old muzhik with a disheveled beard was doing something, bent over some iron [*нагнулся над железом* (9.370)], muttering [*приговаривал*] meaningless French words, and, as always in this nightmare (here lay its terror), she felt that this little muzhik paid no attention to her, but was doing this dreadful thing with iron over her [*в железе над нею*]. And she awoke in a cold sweat. (752)

8. Later that day, confused but determined to find Vronsky, Anna boards a train going in the direction of an estate belonging to Vronsky's mother. At a station she glances out of her window and is startled by the appearance of "a dirty,

---
[2] Richard Gustafson observes that Anna's nightmare "is the only recurrent dream in Tolstoy's fiction" (309).

ugly muzhik in a peaked cap, his matted hair sticking out from under it." He is "bending down to the wheels [*нагибаясь к колесам* (9.385)] of the carriage. 'There's something familiar about that hideous muzhik,' thought Anna" (765).

9. Finally, only a few minutes later, Anna throws herself under the train and is struck on the head by "something huge and implacable" [incapable of appeasement] (*что-то огромное и неумолимое* [9.389]). Simultaneously, "a little muzhik muttering [*приговаривая*] to himself, was working over some iron" (768; *работал над железом* [9.389]).

As is evident, most of the muzhik occurrences bode evil and are more closely connected to Anna:

- a railway watchman is run over and killed by a train;
- the stooping shadow of a man passes under Anna's legs as, simultaneously, the sound of a hammer striking iron rings out;
- a sheet of iron is blown about in a blizzard;
- Anna's nightmare portrays her as trapped in her bedroom while a frightening muzhik leans over a sack groping and chanting French words which conjure up a violent image of beating on iron;
- in Anna's final replay of her nightmare the muzhik pays no attention to her while doing something dreadful "in iron over her";
- and in the last two occurrences again a railroad muzhik worker engages in bending down to the wheels or is working over iron.

The reader senses that each of these occurrences is meaningful and combines with all others to suggest what becomes a *symbol* of a dehumanized grotesquery, disinterestedly wielding malicious, cruel, emotional violence, in this instance, upon Anna.

Symbolism: The Muzhik (Peasant)

I have hypothesized that, by degrees, the repulsive muzhik develops into a *symbol* embodying Anna's perceptions of a debased, dehumanized, grotesque perversion of human love, here exemplified *allegorically* by Karenin and, subsequently, by Vronsky. Several curious aspects of the above nine occurrences must be addressed before such a conclusion appears plausible:

- What is significant about the muzhik speaking French?
- What is the connection between the small, dirty, disheveled, hunched-over muzhik and Karenin/Vronsky?
- Why might Vronsky and Anna have had similar dreams?
- What role could the muzhik's sack play?
- What is so horrifying to Anna about the muzhik's paying no attention to her?
- How do the peasant's French words relate to Anna?
- Preceding Anna's suicide, why does a muzhik seen through a train window seem familiar to her?
- Why is the muzhik's peaked cap significant?
- What role does iron play in the dreams?

Regarding the French-speaking muzhik, many readers have ventured opinions. Most frequently, the assumption is that Vronsky and Anna are disturbed by the muzhik speaking French because the very idea of an uneducated, uncouth muzhik communicating in what the Russian aristocracy considered high style discourse is a grotesquery.[3] Even so, it does seem excessive that a muzhik chanting in French would

---

[3] For example, see Sydney Schultze, who interprets the peasant "who speaks French and works on trains" as a "hideous misfit" (125).

cause the *horror* (rather than merely disgust) both Vronsky and Anna feel while separately contemplating their dreams (355; 361).

My alternate reading is that Vronsky and Anna react strongly to their respective and somewhat similar dreams not because the base peasant inappropriately assumes nobility, but, on the contrary, because they sense that the peasant actually is a debased, dehumanized, grotesque *aristocrat*, now bereft of all nobility, yet still chanting, as it seems, largely incoherent French words. As will be shown below, at the time of Vronsky's and Anna's parallel dreams, the muzhik, in allegorical terms, may recall Vronsky, who, in Anna's eyes — like Karenin before him — has fallen to the level of a small, dirty, crass, disheveled, muzhik.

Invoking the *principle of reasonable probability*, it seems worth exploring whether a previous, similar dehumanization had occurred in Anna's mind before she met Vronsky, that is, at the time she first had this dream "long ago" (361), and "which had come to her *repeatedly* even before her liaison with Vronsky" (752; emphasis added). Prior to her falling in love with Vronsky, could Anna's object of dehumanization have been Karenin? If so, it would be natural for Anna just now to have recalled her dream while Vronsky was cavorting with the foreign prince. At present, she may do so not in order to excoriate Karenin as formerly, but, perhaps subconsciously at this point, because she is horrified that Vronsky may seem to be teetering on the brink of falling into the same odious role of a repulsive, crude, and even emotionally threatening muzhik.

A few minutes earlier, as Vronsky hastens to meet Anna after being absent so long, he nearly bumps into Karenin in the latter's doorway. Vronsky observes Karenin's "bloodless, pinched face under the black hat" and "immobile, dull eyes" peering at him (356). One senses a passing of the baton as

Symbolism: The Muzhik (Peasant)

Vronsky moves by a moribund Karenin[4] and, possibly, into position to assume by degrees the latter's function as muzhik in the peasant dream. That Anna has just recalled this dream while thinking now of Vronsky suggests the possibility that the dream from long ago could acquire a distressing, and even terrifying, new meaning for her.

In a startling reversal a few months later at the time of the birth of Anna and Vronsky's child, Karenin, undergoing a spiritual transformation, assumes a lofty station through "the happiness of forgiveness" (414), while Vronsky now appears "shamed, humiliated, guilty, and deprived of any possibility of washing away his humiliation" (415). Speaking of Karenin and Vronsky, the omniscient narrator remarks that "the roles had been suddenly changed" (415). In context, this refers specifically to Karenin and Vronsky's relative ethical stature, but conceivably also foreshadows Vronsky's replacement of Karenin in the peasant dreams. However, that proposition requires additional support.

A minor and speculative piece of evidence appears early in the novel as a "muzhik with a sack over his shoulder" (60) detrains in Moscow. Although neither Vronsky nor Anna would have understood it, possibly on reflection the *reader* may regard this muzhik as being among the initial images signaling an eventual displacement of Karenin by Vronsky. *Vronsky* observes the muzhik carrying a sack as he gets off the train. If this muzhik at the time allegorically represents a debased Karenin, then his figurative exiting opens a space for Vronsky eventually to enter and, over time, assume the former's role of repugnant muzhik in Anna's dream.

Regarding the muzhik's chanting in *French*, it is relevant that Tolstoy explicitly and on several occasions draws the

---

[4] Gary Adelman views the details in this description as "symbolic forebodings of death" (77).

reader's attention to Karenin's and Vronsky's use of French. As representative examples, recall that the author explicitly states that Karenin communicates with Anna in French at the steeplechase, then when writing to her about the conditions under which she may remain in his house, and while addressing Anna in Betsy's presence before Anna's elopement with Vronsky (210, 212, 283, 424). If anything, the author is even more direct in relation to Vronsky: "He went on in *French*, as he always did, avoiding the impossible coldness of formal Russian and the danger of the informal" (187; emphasis added). In addition, Vronsky later pleads with Anna not to attend the opera, where intolerant, hypocritical society ladies could demean her: "'I ask you not to go, I implore you,' he said *again in French*, with a tender plea in his voice, but with a coldness in his eyes" (543; emphasis added). To Anna, Vronsky is acquiring another attribute of the frightening French-speaking muzhik.

Concerning the question of the similarity of Vronsky and Anna's dreams, I am persuaded that these dreams are fundamentally more coincidental than mystically or metaphysically related.[5] However, they do arise from similar social and psychological stimuli. Vronsky's dream, of which he never speaks a word to Anna, occurs soon after he has recalled the visiting foreign prince's sordid behavior and his own vulgar excesses. Simultaneously, Anna, pregnant by Vronsky and fearing a diminution of his ardor, recalls and relates to her lover a nightmare that is similar to his in several essential features.

---

[5] Alternatively, C.J.G. Turner raises the possibility that Vronsky and Anna's dreams are "sympathetic dreams" of which Schopenhauer wrote in his *Parerga und Paralipomena*. Sympathetic dreams are "ones that are communicated *in distans* and accordingly are dreamed by two people at the same time" (157).

Symbolism: The Muzhik (Peasant)

Consider the context. Before his dream, Vronsky has been away from Anna for a week and too close to the self-indulgent, amoral foreign prince. Feeling disgusted at his recent debauchery, Vronsky acknowledges to himself, "either because he himself had changed lately, or because he had been much too close to this prince [*слишком большая близость с этим принцем* (8:415)], this week seemed terribly burdensome to him" (354).

Recollecting that shameful week and thinking of his imminent meeting with Anna, Vronsky, exhausted, falls asleep. The reader is told that in his mind Vronsky jumbles "thoughts of Anna" and "the muzhik tracker, who had played an important role as a tracker in the bear hunt" (355). In his comparatively uncomplicated dream, Vronsky sees the tracker as probably he recently appeared to him: a small, dirty peasant with a disheveled beard. The peasant is bending down, doing something or other, and "suddenly said some strange words in French." Upon awakening, Vronsky reflects on "the peasant and the incomprehensible French words which the peasant uttered, and horror sent a chill down his spine" (355-56).

Vronsky's dream concretizes the peasant as a "muzhik tracker" [*обкладчик*], one who, Vladimir Dal' explains, "tracks a bear down, locates its lair, and verifies it is in a deep sleep" (2:588), before jabbing it with a long pole and provoking the dazed but enraged bear to emerge into the gun sights of an awaiting hunter.

While falling asleep thinking of Anna, the peasant tracker, and his last week's excesses, Vronsky clearly feels ashamed that he has behaved not as a principled nobleman, but as a banal, base perversion of his station. He seems to have fallen to the level of the "small and dirty" peasant tracker. Possibly, as he anticipates intimacy with Anna, he may view himself at the moment as being far from a noble prince, and, again, as more closely resembling the coarse muzhik tracker. His imagined affirmations quite naturally whispered to Anna *in French* during intimate relations now appear to him less heartfelt and confirming, and more emotionally bereft and brutish, more like what he assumes to be a muzhik's behavior. It is possible (but not demonstrable) that this recognition is what so horrifies Vronsky.

The foregoing interpretation provides realistic motivation for *Vronsky*'s dream. In its proximity to Anna's far more complex, accretive, symbolic nightmares, Vronsky's once-mentioned dream appears devoid of symbol or mysticism, and more coincidental. My assumption is that in Vronsky's case the nightmare arises from the novel's clearly stated realistic stimuli which, nevertheless, are related through logical circumstance to Anna's dream. Both Vronsky and Anna's minds subconsciously and independently settle on a muzhik as the image of human degradation, an association that might easily occur to many of the Russian noble class at the time, surrounded by masses of muzhiks whom they knew poorly and generally considered benighted, devoid of normal human feelings, and even as sub-human creatures. There is no indication that Vronsky and Anna possess the more nuanced and differentiated views which Levin holds in relation to the Russian peasant class.

Compelled to respond to Anna's interrogation about his previous week's dissipation, Vronsky encounters a distraught, jealous woman. Even before their meeting, Tolstoy has described Anna's growing disappointment and anxiety regarding Vronsky. This is first observed following Vronsky's disaster at the steeplechase and her confession to Karenin of her love for Vronsky. Thinking of Vronsky then, Anna "*imagined* that he did not love her, . . . and she felt hostile towards him *because of it*" (287-88; emphasis added). Additionally, Vronsky and Anna's meeting the following day in Vrede's country garden (314-17) increases Anna's apprehension. Upon hearing of Anna's confession to her husband, Vronsky responds with indecision and embarrassed confusion, further alarming Anna.

Just prior to Vronsky's arrival after a week's absence with the prince, Anna vividly *recalls* a dream she had *long ago* [давно уж я видела этот сон (8:423)] culminating in a premonition of death. This death, she now announces to Vronsky, will soon resolve everything: "I will die and deliver myself and you" (361). Completely unaware of Vronsky's dream, Anna recounts to him her clearly remembered and recurring nightmare of long ago, the events of which, she asserts, soon will come to pass and end with her demise. To Vronsky's astonishment and consternation, the dream, in part, parallels and augments his own.

Anna's nightmare is more detailed and, perhaps significantly, takes place in her bedroom, into which she has run "to get something there, to find something out." One could only speculate about what she hopes to get or to find out in her bedroom, but it seems appropriate that from Anna's perspective the dream would take place in her bedroom, not in the study or nursery, just as Vronsky's occurs on a bear hunt. In her bedroom, she encounters a muzhik standing in the corner, again, "with a disheveled beard, small and frightening" (361). He is bent over a sack and gropes around in it with his hands. He, too, mutters in French, but from her dream of long ago Anna clearly remembers his strange, disquieting words: "You must beat the *iron*, pound it, knead it" (361; emphasis added).[6] Vronsky gives no indication of

---

[6] Barbara Lönnqvist plausibly proposes that on one level the muzhik is related to the Russian folkloric blacksmith who "forges destinies, and especially marriages, which is reflected in the songs young women sing when telling their fortune at New Year's Eve" (85). In *Anna Karenina*, however, the symbolic muzhik is French-speaking and closely associated with attributes of compulsion, violence, and death.

connecting these words to his own dream. The symbolic beating on iron image is entirely Anna's.

Furthermore, it seems that Anna's muzhik has no mystical connection to Vronsky's tracker. Her muzhik fumbles and gropes with his hands in a sack, chanting his strange, incoherent, alarming sentence. Although in her telling of the dream, while seeming merely to observe this scene, she also appears somehow to be *trapped inside it, inside the sack*: "I wanted to run away, *but* he bent over a sack and rummaged in it with his hands" (emphasis added) [*Я хотела бежать, но он нагнулся над мешком и руками что-то копошится там* (8.424)]. The word "but" appears to be significant. She wants to escape, *but* is prevented. This suggests Anna's involuntary participation in what was occurring with or within the sack. Her muzhik's French words convey not a precise meaning, but a symbolic aura of cold harshness entirely bereft of human warmth and sensitivity. In every way this impression contradicts the shared emotions natural in normal, assuring, solicitous, mutually fulfilling marital relations.

Consider the French words, "*Il faut le battre le fer, le broyer, le pétrir*," whose English translation is given as "You must beat the iron, pound it, knead it" (361). Among the possible English equivalents listed in the *Larousse Modern French-English Dictionary* are the following: *battre*: beat, thrash, strike, flail, hammer, drive, ram down; *broyer*: crunch, pulverize, grind, mill, pound, crush; and *pétrir*: knead, mold. Little imagination is required to form from these words a semantic field consonant with cold defilement of human intimacy.

Anna relates to Vronsky the last part of her dream, in which her servant Korney claims her death will occur in childbirth. She accepts this interpretation and communicates as much to Vronsky. But soon when this prediction does not come true — although after giving birth, Anna teeters on the very

Symbolism: The Muzhik (Peasant)

brink of death — she recovers, and the dream continues to recur. She must wonder about other interpretations for the French-speaking muzhik. For Anna these possibilities gradually will coalesce into Vronsky's image.

This puzzling sack image occurs only on one other brief occasion very early in the novel, at the time a muzhik gets off a train with a sack over his shoulder (60). In the later, more important manifestation of Anna's dream immediately preceding her suicide, the sack is entirely missing. However, the sack does not disappear from Tolstoy's mind. In his 1886 "Death of Ivan Ilych," the sack (мешок [12.113]) reappears as a symbolic image associated with the darkness and agony of death. Then, at the final moment, through the bottom of the sack, the light of rebirth breaks forth. This may suggest one layer of meaning for the *Anna Karenina* sack. Perhaps in her dream of the muzhik groping about in a sack, Anna most keenly experiences terror at the perceived imminence of the death to occur, as she believes, at the time of her giving birth. When Anna recovers from her near-death, the sack disappears from her later muzhik dreams, replaced by the image of a muzhik not only chanting about a need to beat, pound, and knead iron, but also bending over iron, bending down to the train wheels, or working over iron.

Vronsky's tentative association with the muzhik image striking iron arises already at the Bologovo station as Anna returns to St. Petersburg after assisting Dolly to forgive Stiva. Only a few lines after the "huddled *shadow* of a man slipped under her feet, and there was the noise of a hammer striking iron," the narrator mentions that, although Vronsky "was standing in the shadow, . . . she could see the expression of his face and eyes" (102; emphasis added). Thus the shadowy man who slips under Anna's feet and Vronsky standing in the shadow appear in close proximity. Although not explicit, it is possible that the shadowy figure and Vronsky coalesce as the clanging on iron rings out, foreshadowing even at this early moment a cold hardness that threatens Anna and Vronsky's future relationship.

There is additional background that bears on Anna's nightmare and connects Karenin and Vronsky in her dreams. Recall the dream Anna had after falling in love with Vronsky and entering with him into an adulterous relationship. Tolstoy presents their first sexual union as parallel to Anna's violent death: Vronsky "felt what a murderer must feel when he looks at the body he has deprived of life" (149). Also feeling responsible, Anna begins experiencing a very different, recurring dream "almost every night" (150). In this dream, *both* Karenin and Vronsky figure as her husbands. At this point, far from appearing as repulsive, coarse muzhiks, they both "lavished their caresses on her" (150) [*оба расточали ей свои ласки* (8:179)] and both are contented. Here, "when she had no power over her thoughts," Anna sublimates her shameful behavior and dilemma. Both Karenin and Vronsky caress her. She need not choose between them, or endure pangs of conscience, societal opprobrium, or personal humiliation because of them. Presumably this constitutes Anna's "dream" solution. In it Anna idealizes both lovers, as with equal excess she will come to demonize them later.

However, in real life, Anna must choose between Karenin and Vronsky, the outcome made predictable by her surging passion for Vronsky and her real but increasingly exaggerated disdain for Karenin. Her attempts to condemn Karenin ("he has been stifling my life for eight years" [292]) are both supported and contradicted within the novel. Two examples of the latter follow. On the day of the steeplechase Anna tells Vronsky that Karenin

> 'is not a man, he's a machine, and a wicked machine when he gets angry,' she added, recalling Alexei Alexandrovich in all the details of his figure, manner

of speaking and character, holding him guilty for everything bad she could find in him and forgiving him nothing, *on account of the terrible fault for which she stood guilty before him.* (189; emphasis added)

Here Tolstoy indicates that to a considerable degree Anna's disdain for her husband arises from her own "terrible fault," rather than from his culpability alone.

Second, even more important and clear, Anna expresses her feelings to her husband and others at the birth of her and Vronsky's daughter. Anna is near death and, it seems, for a brief moment all logical and emotional pretense and delusion have vanished. She coolly offers this assessment to her husband:

> She [the other Anna] fell in love with that man [Vronsky], and I [the other Anna] wanted to hate you and couldn't forget the other one [the real Anna] who was there before. The one who is not me [that other Anna (*Та не я*. {8.483})]. Now I'm real, I'm whole. (412)

For a time she is the former Anna, the one who again is pledged and true to Karenin.

Near the end of the novel, on the morning of her suicide, Anna again experiences her peasant dream: a dreadful nightmare, *which had come to her repeatedly even before her liaison with Vronsky,* came to her again" (752; emphasis added; *несколько раз повторявшийся ей в сновидениях еще до связи с Вронским* [9:370]). While recognizing that "even before her liaison with Vronsky" could possibly refer to a time after Anna had met Vronsky but before their sexual union,[7] it seems more likely to me that the dream she had *long ago*

---

[7] For example, later in the novel, Tolstoy uses the word "liaison" to refer to a time before Anna and Vronsky's sexual intimacy: Anna "remembered his words, the expression on his face, like an obedient pointer, in the early days of their *liaison*" (762; emphasis added [*связь* {9.382}]).

(361) first occurs while Anna lives with Karenin before meeting Vronsky. In part, this dream conditions her readiness and rationale for abandoning the disgusting "muzhik" Karenin and entering into an illicit relationship with Vronsky. What follows in the novel just before Anna's suicide is a significant restatement of that much earlier, recurring muzhik dream, this time more clearly referencing Vronsky:

> A little old muzhik with a disheveled beard was doing something, bent over some iron, muttering meaningless French words, and, *as always* in this nightmare (here lay its terror), she felt that this little muzhik *paid no attention to her*, but was doing this dreadful thing with iron over her. And she awoke in a cold sweat. (752; emphasis added) [Она чувствовала, что мужичок этот не обращает на нее внимания, но делает это какое-то страшное дело в железе над нею. И она проснулась в холодном поту]. (9:370)

In part, this Russian passage may be translated literally as "this little muzhik pays no attention to her, but does this certain dreadful act *in iron over her*" (emphasis added).

Again the peasant has a tangled beard as in the earlier version of both Anna's and Vronsky's nightmares. Again the muzhik bends over and does something terrible *in iron* over her, as though he were shrouded or encased in iron and, hence, cold, hard, and incapable of tender feelings. Again he mutters seemingly senseless words in French. Significantly, the reader now learns that as always what makes the dreams so terrifying is that the peasant *pays no attention* to Anna while performing his dreadful act over her in iron.

Much earlier, Anna had told Vronsky that he is her real husband and Karenin "doesn't exist" (188). It has been a long time since the two husbands caressed her in her dreams. Near the end of Anna's life only Vronsky remains, though frustrated with what he considers Anna's erratic, volatile,

Symbolism: The Muzhik (Peasant)

inexplicable behavior. It is precisely at this moment that Anna again experiences her recurring nightmare of the muzhik. Now the reader first learns that the muzhik was doing something dreadful to her in iron over her while *paying no attention to her* (752). Exactly at this moment, the reader observes, Vronsky concludes that he has tried in every way to please Anna and "the only thing left is to pay no attention" (753; emphasis added). The muzhik and Vronsky now treat her in an identical fashion.

If Anna "long ago" dreamt of the repulsive French-speaking peasant while still living as a wife with Karenin even before meeting Vronsky, one may infer that the dream initially portrays Karenin as the repulsive peasant, while later it also embodies Vronsky. A small but telling clue associating Karenin with the stooping peasant beating iron occurs as Karenin confiscates Anna and Vronsky's correspondence and accuses Anna of behaving shamefully because "you must satisfy your animal passions" (364). Anna, in turn, upbraids Karenin for his mean-spirited accusations and evident wish "to hit someone who is down" [бить лежачего (8:427)], as does the muzhik striking iron.

Additional corroborating details also suggest Vronsky's gradual metamorphosis as his relationship with Anna deteriorates into the nightmare's peasant with the disheveled beard. Early in the novel Vronsky is depicted as "a dark, sturdily-built man of medium height" with a "freshly shaven chin" [свежевыбритый подбородок (50; 8:64)]. He could have had a moustache, but none is yet mentioned. At the time of the steeplechase, however, the author does indicate for the first time that Vronsky sports a moustache (313 [усы 8:368]). Also nearer the time of Anna's final dream, as she calls Vronsky home from the nobility elections using the ruse of their daughter's illness, the reader is told that Vronsky wipes his wet beard with a handkerchief (667) [отерев платком *мокрую бороду* (9:274)]. Physically the bearded Vronsky in this detail comes progressively more to resemble the peasant of Anna's nightmare. The *two Alekseis*, Karenin and Vronsky, both of whom increasingly focus more on their own interests than on Anna, appear ever more similar.

Vronsky further resembles the muzhik as he returns early from the nobility elections to assist Anna with the supposedly ill Annie. Upon arriving, Vronsky learns that his daughter has recovered and that Anna, too, is well. He thus assumes he has been deceived. Then, late at night, "seeing that she was again in full possession of him," Anna insists on going with him to Moscow, regardless of the awkwardness of her societal position. Although Vronsky replies that he wants her company, his eyes are those of "a persecuted and embittered man," who senses an approaching disaster. Anna sees this look, which produces only a "momentary impression, but she never forgot it" (668). Now, perhaps, Anna can more clearly see Vronsky as a potential embodiment of the frightening muzhik from her nightmares. However, at the time that impression remains only vague.

Shortly before her suicide, Anna receives a note from Vronsky in response to her urgent appeal that he immediately return to her, for she is frightened about what otherwise might occur. His hastily written reply informs her that he cannot return before evening. Again exasperated, Anna thinks of Vronsky, "I've never hated anyone as I do this man!" (761). At this point, Vronsky not only displaces Karenin, but exceeds him as the most despised figure in Anna's life. As she had loved Vronsky the more, she now despises him the more. Vronsky thus continues his descent to a fuller allegorical identification with the muzhik.

At this time, Anna clearly recalls her bitter disappointment in her *two* loves. Again she reflects on both Karenin and Vronsky. She thinks first of *Karenin* and "remembering the

Symbolism: The Muzhik (Peasant)

feeling there had been between them, which was also called love, she shuddered with disgust" (764) [*вздрогнула от отвращения* (9:383)], as though simultaneously recalling the repugnant muzhik. Anna also considers *Vronsky*, and the narrator reveals her similar reaction: "And with disgust [*с отвращением* (9.384)] she remembered what it was that she called 'that love'" (764) with Vronsky. Anna has arrived at the opposite pole from her much earlier dream when both Karenin and Vronsky were her husbands and both "lavished their caresses on her" (150). The two men in her life now are both consigned to realms inhabited by the repulsive French-speaking muzhik.

It is precisely at this point, having just felt such revulsion for *both* Karenin and Vronsky, her "two husbands" (764), that out of her train window Anna notices a "dirty, ugly muzhik . . . bending down [*нагибаясь*] to the wheels of the carriage." She recognizes that "there's something familiar about that hideous [*безобразный*] muzhik." At this moment, Anna again recalls her dream of the frightening muzhik and trembles with fear (765).

Why at this instant does Anna remember her muzhik dream? What is it that is "familiar about that hideous muzhik" seen through her train window? It seems significant that in outward appearance this current muzhik does not much resemble the muzhik from Anna's former dreams. He is not described as a little man with a disheveled beard. Rather, her attention is drawn to his face. He is ugly [*уродливый*; misshapen, deformed] and his "matted hair" [*спутанные волосы*] sticks out from under a peaked cap [*фуражка*].

Of all the defining elements, what is most important is that the muzhik wears a peaked (military) cap, which is exactly the kind of hat Vronsky wore when Anna first met him and he made such a favorable impression on her:

Recall that while Anna returns to St. Petersburg after reconciling the Oblonskys, she detrains to breathe the fresh, wintery air at the Bologovo station. Vronsky approaches her dressed in a "military greatcoat" and, "putting his hand to his visor, he bowed to her" (102) [*приложив руку к козырьку, он наклонился перед ней* (8.124)] . As expected, Vronsky, in full uniform, also wears his *furazhka* with visor.

Similar to all the muzhiks in Anna's recurring dream, the latter one is "bending down" [*нагибаясь*] to the wheels of the train car. Anna realizes that this muzhik in his peaked cap looks familiar and, "*recalling her dream*, she stepped away to the opposite door, trembling with fear" (765; emphasis added). Very important, Anna, herself, has just linked the muzhik pounding on iron — that is, on a realistic level, testing the soundness of the heavy train wheels — to the muzhik of her nightmare, now wearing a Vronsky-like *furazhka*. At this juncture, the *symbolic* dimension becomes especially prominent. The ugly muzhik in a *furazhka* becomes fully associated in Anna's mind with the unfeeling, cold-blooded, ever-pursuing figure of her imminent death. The muzhik bending over iron in five separate occurrences (3, 6, 7, 8, and 9 of the nine occurrences listed at the beginning of this chapter) and Vronsky himself come into focus in the fundamental symbol of a repulsive, French-speaking, violent, death-conveying, grotesquery that pays no attention to her, regardless of her critical need for near constant, tender, solicitous attention.

The "torn-off sheet of iron" (103) careening in the violent wind at the Bologovo station now *symbolically* seems to reflect a terrible, menacing, death-bearing peril shrouding a cosmic ill-will, of which Vronsky is only one manifestation. Anna has convinced herself that she no longer can hope for a warm, caring, sensitive companion. Like Karenin before him, Vronsky now, in Anna's deforming imagination, stoops over her as a repugnant, indifferent, groping abomination uttering meaningless, insincere, and, thus, abhorrent French words, and, devoid of tender human sensitivity and heart-felt emotion, figuratively striking her. He and she seem far from being tender lovers. They feel encased in iron [в железе над нею (9:370)]. The typifying and essential feature which Anna now intuits as a symbolic image for the whole of her relationships with her two 'husbands' is Karenin and Vronsky's *perceived* unfeeling, coarse, even emotionally brutish defilement of sexual intimacy. The parallel *symbol* of a small, disheveled, grimy muzhik stooping over and beating with a hammer against iron strengthens the suggestion both of emotional defilement and of deathly violence. This wrenching disillusionment is more than Anna can bear. Death appears to be her only fate and recourse. Through it, she will "punish him [Vronsky] and be rid of everybody and of myself" (768). Her "bad omen" perceived at the time the watchman was run over by a train car finally merges with her own grisly demise.

Like every human being, Karenin and Vronsky possess significant weaknesses *and* strengths, irrespective of Anna's perceptions. However, it is finally Anna who crushes her once starry idealizations of Karenin and subsequently of Vronsky in the crucible of severe disappointments. This idealizing/

degrading cycle, in which to a degree every human being participates, is particularly extreme in Anna. Thus, it is one thing for Anna, returning home from reconciling Dolly and Stiva, to be somewhat alarmed at the previously unnoticed "cartilage of [Karenin's] ears"[8] (104), yet she also experiences disappointment upon seeing her son, whom she has every reason to love, but Anna "had imagined him better than he was in reality" (107). Similarly, as Vronsky approaches her after his week with the foreign prince, Anna scrutinizes him through the lens of disillusionment: for "*at every meeting, she was bringing together her imaginary idea of him (an incomparably better one, impossible in reality) with him as he was*" (357; emphasis added).

While Wasiolek correctly views the peasant of Anna's nightmares as ultimately a "symbol of the remorseless, impersonal power of sex" (153), I have proposed that the peasant further symbolizes both Karenin's *and* Vronsky's degradation, largely through Anna's exaggeration of their real and substantial faults, and her subsequent mental debasement of their love for her, characterized in one way as "paying no attention to her." Anna encapsulates their perceived grotesqueness in a perversion of physical intimacy with her, now bereft of affirming sincerity and responsive tenderness toward her. As Anna perishes under the train's massive *iron* wheels, the men in her life fully merge with the final stooping muzhik who mutters something while "working over some iron" (768) [*работал над железом* (9:389)]. She now believes that these men, their emotional essence encased in iron, also regard her as an inanimate, unfeeling, iron-like object. Thus Anna considers herself unappreciated, unloved, and emotionally battered.

---

[8] Gary Saul Morson perceptively comments that "Tolstoy makes it evident that Anna from this point on, *teaches* herself to see Karenin as repulsive and unfeeling" (Anna Karenina *In Our Time* 84).

Symbolism: The Muzhik (Peasant)

To a considerable extent, Anna is ruined by her fateful tendency to despise those around her as she grows too aware of their perceived inadequacies, especially of their inability or unwillingness to devote themselves nearly exclusively to her need for constant emotional and physical gratification. Readers will recall that at one of the novel's most significant moments, Anna yearns to accept but ultimately declines a powerful antidote to her suffering which is offered her by Dolly Oblonskaya, Anna's sister-in-law and true friend: "When you love someone, you love the whole person, as they are, and not as you'd like them to be" (614) [*если любишь, то любишь всего человека, какой он есть, а не каким я хочу, чтоб он был* (9:211)]. Relating to Anna, this wise and powerful observation could well serve as a cautionary epigraph to the entire novel.

Yet, rejecting Dolly's, and presumably Tolstoy's, ethical alternative, Anna yields to her embellishing, then deforming fantasies, which culminate in disillusionment and despair, and in her tragic death beneath the *symbolic* and quintessentially impassive, insensitive, merciless iron mass, something cosmically "*huge and implacable*" (768; emphasis added) [*огромное, неумолимое* (9:389)]. On a metaphysical level Anna utilizes the *iron* train as an implement for vengeance upon society, her two abhorrent French-speaking muzhik husbands, and on herself.

Taken together, the train cluster of symbols — the storm with its wild violence, the knife severing bonds for escape and indulgence, the huge and implacable force, and especially the repellant muzhik — portray Anna's perilous emotional and moral confusion. This weakness is reflected in an inability to find and maintain lasting fulfillment with several others in her life. Her dissatisfaction arises in part from the deficiencies of others in her personal, family, and societal relationships, and in larger part from her own failure to manage extravagant expectations and desires — her inability to remain grounded in the everyday, prosaic realities of life as most of us experience them most of the time. Regarding Anna's culpability, this dissatisfaction appears to be an outcome of her unbridled imagination, dark romantic fantasy, distortion of reality, willing escape into delirium, and, finally, deceit, jealousy, spite, and vengeance. It represents a battle between restraint and propriety on the one hand, early seen in the symbolic image of the cold post, and, on the other, life forces struggling to tear free and soar, suggested by an instrument of severance, the knife.[9]

---

[9] Caryl Emerson convincingly argues for two additional determinates in Anna's tragedy: her sincere but "powerfully mistimed love" and an inability to take the "first steps" toward resolving her painfully difficult situation; that is, her unwillingness "to sign on" – to accept responsibility and act decisively (169-75).

Chapter 3

ALLEGORY: THE STEEPLECHASE PARTICIPANTS

The second major cluster of images, this time less symbolic and more allegorical, emerges from the steeplechase, compactly described on four pages of *Anna Karenina*, part 2, chapter 25. While Anna and her attributes are central in the cluster of symbols introduced through the train ride from Moscow to St. Petersburg, in the steeplechase the greater share of attention is directed toward Vronsky and his character. It is he who rides in the race and alone causes Frou-Frou's death. Yet Anna does play a considerable role on the race's allegorical level through her proxy Frou-Frou, as, to a lesser degree, do Karenin and Seryozha through the horse Gladiator and his rider Makhotin.

Of course, Vronsky is the only one of the four characters to appear in the steeplechase entirely as himself, Frou-Frou's rider, and is the person about whose weaknesses the reader learns most. They include, primarily, his "failure to keep pace" with Anna seen in his awkward movements (responses) at critical moments; insensitivity to Anna's deepest needs; and excessive self-absorption and pride.

Virtually every alert reader observes that Anna participates vicariously in the steeplechase as Vronsky's mount, Frou-Frou. As discussed in greater detail in chapter five below, it is clear already in the novel's first draft that Tolstoy intends for Vronsky's horse, in the beginning named Tani, to stand proxy for that draft's heroine, Tania. In the final version, Frou-Frou and Anna assume corresponding roles.

Allegory: The Steeplechase Participants

For example, in the novel both the dark bay [reddish-brown] horse (181)[1] Frou-Frou and Anna are excited and tremble before the race (182, 186-87). Vronsky straightens "a strand of her mane that had fallen on the wrong side of [Frou-Frou's] sharp withers" (182), reminiscent of Anna's "willful little ringlets of curly hair that adorned her, always coming out on her nape and temples" (79). Later, after Vronsky has broken his mount's back, Frou-Frou falls, "fluttering on the ground at his feet like a wounded bird" (199). Meanwhile, in the stands Anna begins "thrashing about like a trapped bird" (210). Most important, Vronsky's unforgivable "awkward movement" causes both Frou-Frou's death and contributes significantly to Anna's demise three years later. Finally, the name Frou-Frou apparently derives, for the most part,[2] from a contemporary French play popular in Russia written by Henri Meihac and Ludovic Halevy entitled *Frou-Frou* (1869), in which the heroine, Frou-Frou, abandons her husband and son for a lover (Eikhenbaum 190).

Since the steeplechase quite clearly features this allegorical association between Frou-Frou and Anna, the *principle of reasonable probability* suggests that other named steeplechase participants also could have allegorical dimensions. Since Vronsky already is in the race as himself, the reasonable probability is that the other important figures in Anna's life play roles with her in the steeplechase. In fact, most notably Karenin and Seryozha do.

---

[1] Cf. the much later description of Vronsky's horse as Dolly arrives for a visit in the country: Vronsky again is riding an excited and unrestrainable "dark bay thoroughbred" (610).

[2] As Edwina J. Cruise convincingly shows, the novel's steeplechase "is modeled after real-life races, real-life horses, and, most notable in the early drafts, real-life riders." Further, at one point Tolstoy owned a race horse named Frou-Frou, which previously had been entered in the Emperor's Cup at Tsarskoe Selo, but withdrawn before she could compete against Gladiator and others. (Cruise, 1-4)

The largely allegorical parallels between Karenin and the horse Gladiator are similarly clear, although less obvious than those between Anna and Frou-Frou. In order to establish the linkage of Karenin to Gladiator, it is necessary to begin with the early scene of Anna's arrival back in Petersburg following her reconciliation of Dolly with Stiva in Moscow. Upon catching sight of her husband, Anna's first thought is "what's happened with his ears?" She notices the "cartilage of his ears[3] propping up the brim of his round hat," "big weary eyes," and "high voice" (104).

For his part, Vronsky simultaneously observes Karenin's "sternly self-confident figure, his round hat and slightly curved back. . . . The gait [*походка*] of Alexei Alexandrovich, swinging his whole pelvis and his blunt feet, was especially offensive to Vronsky" (105). Each of these features will link Karenin to Gladiator at the steeplechase. During the race, Vronsky is offended by Gladiator's "wonderful hindquarters" [*чудесный зад*] which "bobbed steadily and easily just in front of Vronsky" (197). These rhythmically gyrating hindquarters taunt Vronsky during much of the race — as earlier Karenin's "swinging his whole pelvis" (105) seemed to mock Vronsky.

On the day of the steeplechase, Vronsky's roommate remarks, "They say Makhotin's Gladiator has gone lame," possibly an oblique reference to Karenin's impaired relationship with Anna. But Vronsky, as though acknowledging that Karenin still is in a position of undiminished legal, political, and societal authority, merely replies "Nonsense!" (179). Further, Vronsky tells Frou-Frou's trainer that Gladiator is "my one serious rival" (181), as also is Karenin, *legally* married to

---

[3] In draft seven (n.d.) Tolstoy crosses out the following description of Karenin: "his tall, full figure with a hat pulled straight down onto his broad, intelligent, brow . . ." (Толстой, Полное 20: 189). Consequently the way becomes open for Karenin's large ears to appear prominently in the final version.

Allegory: The Steeplechase Participants

Anna. On his way to Frou-Frou just before the race begins, Vronsky sees the "big-eared" Gladiator (192, 194) and the horse's "large, exquisite, perfectly regular form, with wonderful hindquarters and unusually short pasterns [бабки] sitting just over the hoof" (194). Again, recall Karenin's "swinging his whole pelvis and his blunt feet" (105). *Immediately* after this description of *Gladiator*, a spectator exclaims to Vronsky, "Ah, there's *Karenin*" (194), who appears to complement his equestrian alter ego, complete, the reader learns, with a "black hat and so-familiar ears sticking out of it" (204), and the "big, round hat that pressed down the tops of his ears" (207), recalling the "big-eared" Gladiator. A colleague facetiously asks Karenin whether he is racing today, to which he replies meaningfully, "Mine is a harder race." The omniscient author disingenuously remarks that this "reply did not mean anything" (209), although in fact it merges the steeplechase with Karenin's actual "race" to win back and secure Anna's loyalty.

Why might Karenin, like Anna, be associated with a horse? In one important way the answer appears to lie in Vronsky, on whom the steeplechase centers. Immediately before the race, Vronsky visits Anna and learns she is pregnant with their child. He feels chagrined that he and Anna have concealed their relations from Karenin for so long (188). According to Vronsky's code as an officer of the Imperial Guard, an offended husband has the right to demand satisfaction through a duel. But Anna and Vronsky have hidden their affair from Karenin. Feeling duplicitous toward the socially upright and politically powerful Karenin, Vronsky now races Karenin in the form of Gladiator (one who duels) and thus figuratively battles his opponent. Thus, Karenin runs in the steeplechase as Gladiator, as well as throughout the novel, more significantly, in a lengthy, punishing race against Anna's lover.

The thought that Karenin could participate in the steeplechase, writes critic V. Ermilov, "is, of course, ludicrous" (26). However, he does allow that Karenin races in the novel's subtext, for both he and Vronsky are "knocked from the saddle" during this contest. Ermilov explains that Anna delivers a sharp blow to her husband through her indiscretion in the stands during the race and her confession to Karenin afterwards. But if, in addition, the horse Gladiator allegorically represents Karenin, Anna's husband figuratively does compete against Vronsky in the steeplechase, as well as in his family. Gladiator gallops past Vronsky and "wins" the steeplechase, just as Karenin temporarily does in relation to Anna and to society following the steeplechase. In the stands, Karenin insists that Anna return home with him. Finally, "Anna glanced fearfully at him, obediently stood up and placed her hand on her husband's arm" (211). The next day Karenin also triumphs in his governmental rivalries, his success proving "even greater than he had expected." Awakening the following morning, Karenin "recalled with pleasure the previous day's victory and could not help smiling" (318).

Directly before and during the steeplechase, Gladiator's rider Makhotin also plays a mildly important role as Seryozha's allegorical surrogate. Before the race Vronsky tells his dissolute companion Yashvin that "Makhotin's the only danger" (177). Approaching the starting post, Vronsky at first does not see "his chief rival, Makhotin on Gladiator" (195). Then Makhotin trots past Vronsky, upsetting Frou-Frou: "Makhotin smiled, showing his long teeth, but Vronsky gave him an angry look. [Vronsky] generally did not like him and now considered him *his most dangerous rival*, and he was vexed that the man had ridden past, alarming his horse" (196; emphasis added). Vronsky earlier had designated the horse Gladiator as his "one serious rival" (181), while now he also claims the rider Makhotin is his "chief rival" (195),

Allegory: The Steeplechase Participants

thus combining horse and rider into his principal threat, as are Karenin and Seryozha in the "real-life" race for Anna's devotion.

During the race, it is Makhotin who confounds Vronsky and Frou-Frou's strategy to pass Gladiator next to the inside rope, the shortest course around the track. Significantly, just prior to the steeplechase the reader learns it is mainly Seryozha who disturbs Anna and Vronsky's peace of mind: "This boy was a more frequent hindrance to their relations than anyone else" (185). Further, Seryozha serves as a compass showing Vronsky that "the direction in which he is swiftly moving diverges widely from his proper course" (186). Finally during the race itself, Vronsky allows Frou-Frou to decide when to make her move, and she passes Makhotin and Gladiator on the slope before the next obstacle, possibly an allusion to Anna's approaching decision, following her recovery from a serious illness contracted soon after Annie's birth, to leave Seryozha behind and flee abroad with Vronsky.

Of all those in the race, now only Vronsky and Frou-Frou run ahead of Makhotin on Gladiator. It is Vronsky and Frou-Frou who, at present, kick mud back at the latter. However, as the reader has learned just before the race, Vronsky is feeling duplicitous in relation to Karenin (Gladiator) and beginning to acknowledge his guilt before Seryozha (Makhotin). During the race, Vronsky notices Makhotin's curious, mud-bespattered, smiling face (198). Within the allegory, Makhotin (the name may remind the Russian reader of "makhon'kii" [*маxoнький*], a Russian colloquialism for "small") represents a currently young and naïve boy, who, in due time, will become more fully cognizant of his mother's and Vronsky's behavior. Though Makhotin temporarily is in second place, his smile may presage Seryozha's hope of recovering prominence in Anna's heart. This smile may also ridicule Vronsky, who believes he is able to overtake and permanently displace Seryozha in the race for Anna's love. Vronsky will never fully win that race, as Tolstoy has shown through the image of the compass: Vronsky and Anna have diverged from the right course and are rushing toward awaiting disaster.

The *principle of reasonable probability* might lead to further speculation regarding the only other *named* horse and rider out of the seventeen pairs in the steeplechase. Less textual evidence connects the most likely candidates, Princess Betsy and her current lover Tushkevich (134), to the steeplechase participants Diana and Kuzovlev. Nevertheless, at the *first* barrier it is Kuzovlev who "let go of the reins after the leap" causing him and his horse Diana to fly "head over heels." Now he lies "floundering with Diana on the other side of the stream" (197). The parallel appears to be of the inconstant Tushkevich and Betsy, who have no intention of making or maintaining any serious commitments to one another, nor, as Kuzovlev and Diana, any intention to surmount obstacles or continue the difficult race. Kuzovlev reveals his shallowness at the very beginning of the steeplechase, an allegorical representation of a race for a *sincere, enduring love*. Now fallen, he and Diana merely wallow in the mud of their alter-egos' debauchery. A second later, Frou-Frou appears to be in danger of landing on Diana and suffering her same fate. But "like a falling cat" and "straining her legs and back" (197), Frou-Frou adjusts in mid-air and deftly averts this hazard. Anna's behavior, while immoral, is not entirely superficial or ephemeral, as is that of Tushkevich and Betsy. At the beginning, Anna and Vronsky appear willing to commit their all to preserving, strengthening, and defending their deepening relationship.

In addition, the reader soon learns that prior to the race Princess Betsy (Diana) and Anna (Frou-Frou) have placed their bets on the feckless Kuzovlev (Tushkevich). Why would Tolstoy include this ostensibly irrelevant and superfluous detail? Even if Betsy favors Kuzovlev, why would *Anna* concur? One possible answer may be that Anna wishes to deflect attention from her inward cheering for Vronsky. If so, she does not help herself by so obviously following Vronsky's every move during the race, and by her display of horror and despair as he falls. In an additional allegorical sense, Anna may bet on Kuzovlev because she now is most comfortable in Betsy's circle and knows of Betsy's liaison with Tushkevich. Anna already tacitly approves of their trivial romantic attachment. She appears to be in accord with Betsy and Tushkevich (Diana and Kuzovlev) and following in their tracks. Yet, as in the steeplechase, Anna (Frou-Frou) presently "leaps" far beyond them, also in emotional sincerity, seriousness, and depth.

Later in the novel when Vronsky is reluctant to accompany Anna to the opera, where, indeed, she will suffer a painful affront, it is upon the fickle Tushkevich that she places her hopes, reflecting the depths to which she has sunk. He agrees to escort her to the theater. This slight reference does provide at least another tenuous link to the Diana/Kuzovlev and Betsy/Tushkevich pairs. If, as I have suggested, the allegorical steeplechase parallels life's race for a genuine, unwavering, fulfilling love, the hypocritical, hedonistic Diana and Kuzolev fail at the first obstacle and fall out of contention, as they soon do out of "love." Vronsky and Anna, with their illicit but, for a considerable period, sincere and resilient love, avoid society's tedious debauchery and continue the fatal contest.

So many other prominent society figures in *Anna Karenina* appear in passing to relate to horses[4] and, by implication,

---

[4] Implicit similarities between a number of *Anna Karenina*'s characters and horses appear throughout the novel. For example, when Stiva Oblonsky awakens at the beginning of the novel, his servant stands nearby holding his master's shirt "like a horse collar" (6). As Anna arrives by train in St. Petersburg, she bids Countess Vronsky farewell and "went out with a quick step [походка], which carried her rather full body with such strange lightness" (63). Later in Princess Betsy's salon Karenin enters

to the steeplechase that the race properly stands at the allegorical center of the novel's critical mass. In one form or another, much of high society participates in a hopeless race for satisfying love in extra-marital liaisons. An atmosphere of superficially discreet infidelity pervades the novel. Since the actual race is first told primarily from Vronsky's perspective and focuses largely on *his* weaknesses,[5] it is logical to assume that Anna, Karenin, and Seryozha are the implied human referents for the principal allegorical horses and rider in the contest: Frou-Frou (the hesitant, then compliant lover), Gladiator (the powerful rival), and Makhotin (the small but most painful impediment). Beyond Vronsky's personal perceptions, moreover, one observes that Karenin and Seryozha continue in the race, muddied and battered socially and emotionally, but, in a relative sense, ultimate victors in society. They manage to remain comparatively upright, whereas Vronsky and Anna in the end sink deeply into the mud of their illicit indulgence and lose the race, the illusory quest for an idyllic, fulfilling, *extramarital*, love.

"with his calm, clumsy gait" [походка] (140). Preparing to greet her guests, Princess Betsy barely has time after the theater to "sprinkle powder on her long, pale face and wipe it off" (132). Yashvin, Vronsky's closest regimental friend, is described as having "big hands," "enormous legs," and "a long back" (176-77). With her "beautiful, pensive eyes" and "unattractive, yellow face," Countess Lydia Ivanovna consoles a distraught Karenin (508). Also, Natalie Shcherbatsky's husband, Lvov, is described as a man with "curly, shining silver hair" and a "thoroughbred appearance" (682). Finally, the Frenchman Landau, on whom Karenin relies for inspiration to know whether to grant Anna a divorce, is described as "a short, lean man with womanish hips and knock-kneed legs, very pale, handsome, with beautiful, shining eyes and long hair falling over the collar of his frock coat" (732).

[5] To repeat for the reader's convenience, Vronsky's inadequacy includes his "failure to keep pace," that is, his awkward movements (responses) at critical moments; his insensitivity to Anna's deepest needs; and his excessive self-absorption and pride.

Chapter 4

ALLEGORY: THE STEEPLECHASE'S RECURRING MOTIFS

Chapter 4

In order to explore a far more important allegorical dimension of the steeplechase in *Anna Karenina,* it is necessary first to consider a significant feature of the novel's structure. Anna and Vronsky figure prominently in eight *episodes* of the novel. Typically, these episodes are interspersed with others, mainly involving Levin and/or Kitty.

Each successive pair of Anna/Vronsky episodes forms a *sequence,* of which there are four in the novel. Each sequence includes, among much else, a series of six especially important and recurring *motifs* from the steeplechase discussed below. Motif six in each of the four sequences includes Anna's figurative, near, or, finally, literal death.

Subsequent references to sequences and episodes will relate to the following structure.

SEQUENCE 1

Episode 1

In February 1872,[1] Anna travels by train from St. Petersburg to Moscow and back to St. Petersburg. While in Moscow, she reconciles Stiva and Dolly Oblonsky and attends a ball at which she becomes romantically attracted to Vronsky. During the train ride back to St. Petersburg, Anna and Vronsky converse at the Bologovo train station. Their feelings for one another intensify.

---

[1] Here for the most part I follow the chronology ingeniously deduced by Vladimir Nabokov (190-198).

Allegory: The Steeplechase's Recurring Motifs

Episode 2

In St. Petersburg, Anna and Vronsky often meet in Princess Betsy's indulgent social circle. In December 1872, Anna and Vronsky consummate their extra-marital union, at the conclusion of which Anna is portrayed as a murder victim. Anna becomes pregnant in or about April 1873.

SEQUENCE 2

Episode 3

On 15 August 1873, Vronsky breaks Frou-Frou's back in the Peterhof steeplechase. Before the race, Anna tells Vronsky she is pregnant and, after the race, she admits to Karenin that she is Vronsky's mistress. In a meeting at Vrede's garden, Vronsky disappoints Anna by his evident perplexity and indecisiveness.

Episode 4

Vronsky is assigned to host a dissolute foreign prince. Vronsky and Anna each experience similar nightmares about a repulsive French-speaking muzhik. In January 1874, Anna nearly dies in childbirth and Vronsky attempts suicide. Both recover and flee to Europe in March 1874.

SEQUENCE 3

Episode 5

Vronsky and Anna spend from March 1874 through the winter of 1874-75 abroad, mainly in Italy. There they visit the Russian artist Mikhailov.

Episode 6

In March 1875, Vronsky and Anna spend two weeks in St. Petersburg. Anna visits Seryozha on his birthday. Anna is publicly insulted at an opera. Figuratively, crucial sides of Anna "die" as she abandons Seryozha a second time and is "mortified" in society.

SEQUENCE 4

Episode 7

Vronsky and Anna establish residence on Vronsky's country estate and remain there from late March 1875 through November 1875. Dolly visits them briefly in July. Vronsky attends the nobility elections in October. At the end of November, Anna and Vronsky travel to Moscow.

Episode 8

Anna and Vronsky remain in Moscow from late November 1875 until Anna's suicide in May 1876, over four years after the beginning of her fateful attraction to Vronsky.

Returning now to the steeplechase, the course consists of nine obstacles, although Tolstoy focuses only on the start of the race and on five of the nine obstacles. These *six emphases become important recurring motifs* in the novel. They acquire allegorical prominence as they relate to important corresponding obstacles (motifs) throughout the Anna/Vronsky relationship.

Motifs 1, 2, and 6 always begin and end each of the four Anna/Vronsky sequences. By contrast, the order of motifs 3, 4, and 5 is less rigid. They can occur in any order (3, 4, 5; 4, 3, 5; etc.), depending on exigencies of plot. Again, all six motifs are rooted in the actual steeplechase, but produce allegorical resonance as the motifs recur within each of the novel's four Anna/Vronsky sequences. The repeating motifs help define and, again, subtly emphasize Tolstoy's principal moral message in *Anna Karenina.*

Following each of the *six allegorical steeplechase motifs* identified below are the *six parallel Anna/Vronsky motifs* recurring in their relationship. The latter are indented and italicized. As I will demonstrate below, these six Frou-Frou/

Allegory: The Steeplechase's Recurring Motifs

Vronsky motifs introduced in the steeplechase recur within each of the four Anna/Vronsky sequences in the novel. Most readers initially do not notice these unobtrusive repetitions, which subtly reinforce the author's message, perhaps even at the level of the reader's subconscious.

Motif 1. Approaching the starting line, Frou-Frou is *agitated and contrary*: "As if not knowing which foot to put first, Frou-Frou, pulling at the reins with her long neck, started off as if on springs, rocking her rider on her supple back. . . . The excited horse, *trying to trick her rider*, pulled the reins now to one side, now to the other, and *Vronsky tried in vain to calm her* with his voice and hand. . . . Excited and much too high-strung, *Frou-Frou lost the first moment*, and several horses started ahead of her, . . . For the first few minutes *Vronsky was not yet master either of himself or of his horse*. Up to the first obstacle, the stream, he was unable to guide his horse's movements" (195-97; emphasis added).

> *In response to Vronsky's early advances, Anna initially is agitated, hesitant, and resistant. Early in the relationship, Vronsky often appears bewildered and/or inept.*

Motif 2. Frou-Frou rises over the *first obstacle* not far behind the horses Gladiator and Diana, "but just as Vronsky felt himself in the air, he suddenly saw, almost under his horse's feet, Kuzovlev floundering with Diana on the other side of the stream . . . now all [Vronsky] saw was that Diana's leg or head might be *right on the spot where Frou-Frou had to land*. But Frou-Frou, like a falling cat, *strained her legs and back during the leap* and, *missing the horse, raced on*. 'Oh, you sweetheart!' thought Vronsky. After the stream, *Vronsky fully mastered the horse*." (197; emphasis added).

> *Through Anna's agility, Vronsky and Anna avert an early danger to their relationship, the danger of falling into the common mire of a superficial societal liaison. Compared to society in general, Anna deftly eludes shallow promiscuity, thereby permitting her to rationalize her guilty behavior, and, straining, remain relatively upright. Now more settled, Vronsky assumes a prominent, confident role in the relationship.*

Motif 3. At the *big barrier* called the "devil" located in front of the tsar's pavilion where *all of high society*, the devil's court, had gathered, *Frou-Frou clears the boards* "without the least change of movement. . . . the boards vanished, and [*Vronsky*] *only heard something knock behind him*. Excited by Gladiator going ahead of her, the *horse had risen too early* before the barrier and knocked against it with a back hoof. But her pace did not change and *Vronsky, receiving a lump of mud in the face*, realized that he was again the same distance from Gladiator" (198; emphasis added).

> *Vronsky and Anna appear to surmount a societal obstacle to their success, although Anna's slight miscalculation suggests that in her case the obstacle may not be overcome entirely, and Vronsky is bespattered.*

Motif 4. When Vronsky recognizes the best time to pass Makhotin on Gladiator, "Frou-Frou, already knowing his thoughts, speeded up noticeably without any urging," but is blocked by Makhotin/Gladiator from taking an inside position. As Vronsky merely thinks of passing on the outside, "Frou-Frou switched step and started to go ahead precisely that way." Vronsky works the reins, urging Frou-Frou on, and after taking several strides together with Gladiator, "*moves ahead on the downhill slope.*" Still, Vronsky can sense that *Gladiator is close behind him* "and constantly heard just

Allegory: The Steeplechase's Recurring Motifs

at his back the steady tread and the short, still quite fresh breathing of Gladiator's nostrils" (198).

> *Intuiting and accommodating Vronsky's will, Anna, with difficulty, surmounts a serious <u>family obstacle</u> from Karenin and/or Seryozha. Family concerns continue to pursue Anna.*

Motif 5. Vronsky and Frou-Frou surmount the *Irish bank*, "the <u>most difficult" obstacle</u>. To both horse and rider comes "a moment's <u>lack of confidence" in the other</u>. Vronsky even "raised his whip, but felt at once that his doubt was groundless" (198-99).

> *Vronsky and Anna surmount their <u>most difficult obstacle</u>, one <u>within their own relationship</u>. To both comes a momentary lack of trust in the other. Vronsky nearly overreacts, but resists the impulse.*

Motif 6. "*Wishing to come in a long first,*" Vronsky urges Frou-Frou on to victory. "Drawing on her last reserve," Frou-Frou *flies over the easiest obstacle, a small ditch*, "but just then Vronsky felt to his horror that, *having <u>failed to keep up with the horse's movement</u>, he, not knowing how himself, had made a wrong, an unforgivable movement* as he lowered himself into the saddle. . . . The *awkward movement* had broken her back. . . . His face disfigured by passion, pale, his lower jaw trembling, Vronsky *kicked her in the stomach with his heel* . . . She did not move but, burying her nose in the ground, merely looked at her master with her speaking eye" (199-200; emphasis added).

> *Largely due to Vronsky's self-absorption and vanity, he and Anna <u>fail to surmount a relatively minor obstacle in their relationship</u>. Vronsky makes an <u>awkward movement</u> and, in consequence, Anna perishes. As at the beginning of their relationship, Vronsky again appears inept and/or bewildered.*

Before suggesting how the six motifs recur in each of the four Anna/Vronsky sequences, I wish to emphasize certain caveats and provide additional clarification:
- The first motif (hesitation), second motif (overcoming conscience and rationalizing guilt), and sixth motif ("death" at a relatively minor obstacle) begin and end each of the four sequences.
- Motifs 3, 4, and 5 represent overcoming serious obstacles within *society*, *family* (Karenin and / or Seryozha), and *the Anna/Vronsky relationship*, respectively. These three obstacles may appear in any order, depending upon the logic of the novel's plot development within a given sequence.
- A sequence's plot requirements may condition a heavier or lighter emphasis on certain of the six motifs. On occasion the plot may include within the same sequence more than one example of a given motif. This emphasizes the importance of that particular motif in the sequence.
- As the novel progresses, *certain of the obstacles surmounted in the steeplechase are not overcome* in the Anna/Vronsky relationship, signaling the weakening of the Anna/Vronsky bond, a prelude to the appearance of motif 6, death.

Tolstoy's subtle, often virtually subliminal, repetition of the steeplechase's allegorical motifs in the novel's four Anna/Vronsky sequences sensitizes and forewarns the reader of the dangerous course the author considers typical in extra-marital relationships: early hesitation and vacillation before initiating or continuing an extra-marital affair; rationalization of one's illicit behavior; overcoming obstacles to an affair erected by society, one's family, and the new relationship's inevitable incompatibilities; and lastly, when all major barriers appear to be overcome, a gratuitous disaster occasioned by a relatively minor obstacle and owing, essentially, to self-absorption and inattention of one or both within the pair. Despite Anna and Vronsky's apparent and, at least at first, considerable success, Tolstoy incrementally repeats for the reader four times the infidelity pattern of six motifs, revealing a gradual degradation of the relationship, and its final devastating consequences for all concerned.

A summary of relevant aspects of the *four sequences'* plots now follows, referencing the *six allegorical steeplechase motifs* as they appear in each Anna/Vronsky sequence.

Sequence 1, motif 1

Anna initially is agitated and hesitant; Vronsky appears inept and/or bewildered

As expected, the hesitation motif is particularly significant throughout much of the first sequence composed of episodes one and two. When Anna first meets Vronsky, a "surplus of something so overflowed her being that it expressed itself beyond her will." Yet Anna "deliberately extinguished the light in her eyes, but it shone against her will in a barely noticeable smile" (61). Later when Vronsky unexpectedly stops by the Oblonskys' home, Anna sees Vronsky from afar and experiences both a "strange feeling of pleasure" and a "fear of something" (75).

At the formal Moscow ball, Tolstoy offers a memorable metonymy for Anna's increasingly unbridled side through the "willful little ringlets of curly hair that adorned her, always coming out on her nape and temples," defying her attempts at composure and restraint. Yet when Vronsky approaches her, Anna quickly agrees to dance with another partner rather than accept Vronsky's imminent invitation (79). Then, as Kitty observes Anna and Vronsky dancing together, Anna "seemed to be struggling with herself to keep these signs of joy from showing, but they appeared on her face of themselves."

Meanwhile, Vronsky's usual "quiet, firm manner and carefree, calm expression" recede, replaced by an evident desire "to fall down before her, and in his glance there was only obedience [покорность (8:100); submissiveness] and fear" (81). Clearly he, too, is smitten and, for a time, enfeebled.

Traveling by train back to Petersburg, Anna, while thinking of Vronsky, experiences "quick transitions from steaming heat to cold and back to heat" (100). Tempted by Vronsky's allure, Anna at this point still is "able, at will, to surrender to it or hold back from it" (101). In a calm moment, Anna is glad that "tomorrow I'll see Seryozha and Alexei Alexandrovich, and my good and usual life will go on as before" (99). Nevertheless, Vronsky again arouses her passion as they meet during the raging blizzard on a platform of the Bologovo train station. But a few hours later when again back in her own home, Anna feels herself "firm and irreproachable" (109) as she mentally defends Karenin: "all the same, he's a good man, truthful, kind and remarkable in his sphere." Yet when Karenin comes into their bedroom precisely at midnight, Anna's animation disappears: "the fire now seemed extinguished in her or hidden somewhere far away" (112).

Sequence 1, motif 2

Anna deftly deflects blame and rationalizes her guilt;
Vronsky regains composure

After Anna's return to St. Petersburg, she avoids her husband's circle of "governmental, male interests" and Lydia Ivanovna's circle of pious women, the "conscience of Petersburg society," preferring instead Princess Betsy Tverskoy's more indulgent and dissolute circle in the "great world." Here Anna admits to herself that Vronsky's "pursuit not only was not unpleasant for her but constituted the entire interest of her life" (128). By selecting Betsy's circle, Anna adroitly avoids the necessity of dissembling and compromise, and circumvents feelings of guilt, inasmuch as most in Betsy's circle behave with considerably baser moral abandon than does she. As Anna warms to Vronsky, he grows in confidence.

Sequence 1, motif 3

Anna and Vronsky surmount a societal obstacle, although a hint of danger remains

At a soirée, members of Betsy's circle discuss whether one can know love fully without some "mistake" [immorality], followed by "correcting oneself." Suspecting that Anna and Vronsky are on the verge of committing their "mistake," and in the presence of several other society figures, Betsy provocatively solicits Anna's opinion on the matter. Avoiding the pitfall, as did Frou-Frou at the steeplechase when the fallen Diana could have caused her to trip and stumble out of the race, Anna responds: "If there are as many minds as there are men, then there are as many kinds of love as there are hearts." Vronsky had been holding his breath for fear of what Anna might say. Now, relieved by her disarming response, he "exhaled as if after danger when she spoke these words" (138). However, presently Karenin arrives, a reminder of his threatening proximity.

Sequence 1, motif 5

Anna and Vronsky surmount an obstacle within their relationship, although they do experience a momentary lack of trust in each other, and Vronsky nearly overreacts

In sequence 1, motif 5 precedes motif 4. Again, motifs 3, 4, and 5 (overcoming obstacles in society, family, and their own relationship) may appear in any order, depending on plot development. While at Betsy's salon, Anna tells Vronsky "you make me feel guilty of something." She forbids him to speak of love and claims she merely wants to be his good friend, "but her eyes were saying something different."

Seeing those eyes filled with love for him, Vronsky disingenuously and dramatically nearly overreacts, pledging to "disappear" if she wills it.

Anna now must confess that, in truth, she does not wish "to drive [him] away."

As they part later that evening, Vronsky realizes his dangerous maneuver has succeeded: "He had come closer to attaining his goal in that one evening than he had in the past two months" (139-41).

Sequence 1, motif 4

Anna and Vronsky surmount a family obstacle; family continues pursuit

Later, upon returning from Betsy's soirée, Karenin attempts to pierce Anna's "impenetrable armor of lies" (145). He cautions her against violating their marital bonds and disregarding her son, and tells her "I am your husband and I love you."

Taken aback by Karenin's uncharacteristic expression of love, Anna, nevertheless, quickly recovers and assures herself "he doesn't even know what love is" (147). Lying in bed late that night, Anna both fears and hopes Karenin will continue speaking of her perilous situation. When he is silent, she acknowledges to herself she has decided in favor of Vronsky, and is incapable of turning back: "'It's late now, late, late,' she whispered with a smile" (148).

But Karenin and Seryozha will continue to trouble her conscience throughout much of the novel.

Sequence 1, motif 6

Having surmounted many difficult obstacles, Anna and Vronsky fail just as success seems assured; self-absorbed, Vronsky makes an awkward movement and Anna perishes; again Vronsky appears inept and bewildered

As Anna and Vronsky view matters, the most serious obstacles to their illicit happiness appear overcome. Having now just consummated their passion, "that which for almost a year had constituted the one exclusive desire of Vronsky's life, replacing all former desires; that which for Anna had been an impossible, horrible, but all the more enchanting dream of happiness — this desire had been satisfied." But Tolstoy paints a dark picture of their reaction. As at the time of Frou-Frou's death, Vronsky, "pale, his lower jaw trembling," now stands over Anna who, paralleling the end of the steeplechase, "falls from the divan where she had been sitting to the floor at his feet." Her passion now sated, Anna considers *herself* "criminal and guilty," contrasting with Frou-Frou at the steeplechase, where Vronsky is the *sole* cause of his mount's fall. In part parallel to that race, the specter of Anna's death appears as Vronsky "felt what a murderer must feel when he looks at the body he has deprived of life. This body deprived of life was their love, the first period of their love" (149). Anna now recognizes that all from her former life has perished. She voices her apprehension in a solemn warning: "'Everything is finished,' she said, 'I have nothing but you. Remember that.'" For his part, Vronsky, in an "awkward movement," speaks of his joy from "one minute of happiness," to which Anna "with loathing and horror" responds, "what happiness?" (150). If Vronsky now senses what a murderer must feel, Anna, both fulfilled and ashamed, leaves Vronsky "with an expression of cold despair on her face" (150).

Sequence 2, motif 1

Anna initially is agitated and hesitant; Vronsky appears inept and bewildered

Now in sequence 2, all the six motifs recur anew, as they will in sequences 3 and 4.

Vronsky visits Anna at her summer home just before the steeplechase. He is unaware and unprepared for the new level of responsibility awaiting him. Anna is agitated, her lips and hands trembling and face flushed as she considers whether or not to tell Vronsky she is pregnant. Worried that his response to her condition may reflect a lack of understanding of the deep significance for them both, she hesitates before divulging her secret. Although Vronsky's response reflects bewilderment — he "paled, was about to say something, but stopped, let go of her hand and hung his head" — on this occasion Anna gives him an ample benefit of the doubt: "'Yes, he understands all the significance of this event,' she thought, and gratefully pressed his hand" (187-88). Partially recovering, Vronsky suggests that Anna leave her husband and live with him — although the next day his vacillation and bewilderment recur as he frankly asks himself, "Am I ready for that?" (305).

Sequence 2, motif 2

Anna deftly deflects blame and rationalizes her guilt; Vronsky regains composure

As Vronsky suggests that Anna leave her husband, Anna suddenly feels ashamed of her behavior. Contemplating the implications for Seryozha and herself were she to desert Karenin, Anna "withdrew somewhere into herself and another woman stepped forward, strange and alien to him" (189). But then "a wicked light" comes into Anna's eyes and she mockingly impersonates Karenin's probable response were she to tell him of her relations with Vronsky. Although she blames Karenin for everything, the omniscient author reveals that she is deluding herself, disparaging Karenin "on account of the terrible fault for which she stood guilty before him" (189), yet rationalizing her guilt.

At this time, without further thought of Anna, Vronsky confidently completes final preparations for the steeplechase, largely oblivious to Anna's deep heartache.

Sequence 2, motif 4

Anna and Vronsky surmount a family obstacle; family continues pursuit

On the same day, Karenin arrives at Peterhof not long before the steeplechase in order to pay a socially obligatory call on Anna. She fears he may want to spend the night. However, she cheerily greets him "with a gay and radiant face," while recognizing her "already familiar spirit of lying and deceit." Anna disingenuously encourages Karenin to spend the night and even to remain with her here at Peterhof (204-05). However, she is greatly relieved when he declines. Though momentarily successful in her pretense, Anna, to her credit, "could never recall that whole little scene without a tormenting sense of shame" (205).

Furthermore, following Vronsky's fall at the steeplechase and Anna's too obvious despair, Karenin insists on escorting Anna home. While still in her carriage, Anna, disregarding her painful "shame and embarrassment," tells Karenin she loves only Vronsky. Regarding her husband she can only exult, "it's all over with him," although he continues to maintain considerable power over her, demanding that outwardly conventions of propriety be observed (213; 292). Still, the next day she muses, "How well I did to tell him everything" (213).

Sequence 2, motif 5
Anna and Vronsky surmount an obstacle in their relationship, although they experience a momentary lack of trust in each other and Vronsky nearly overreacts

Here, motif 5 is especially important as Anna and Vronsky's relationship is imperiled. This motif occurs twice at this point and once again later in the same sequence. To begin, Anna further justifies her excessive frankness with Karenin, for now at least "there would be no falsehood and deceit" (287). However, late that evening, "terrified of the disgrace" (287), she lacks the confidence to inform Vronsky she has confessed everything to her husband.

On the day after the race, she admits to herself she "wanted to call [Vronsky] back" but feared his reaction. Now she *imagines* that he no longer loves her. This leads to a feeling of hostility towards him and, as she clutches her hair in both hands and painfully presses on her temples, she experiences an anguished sensation that "everything was beginning to go double in her soul" (287-93). Then Anna recovers somewhat and considers herself blameless, for "God has made me so that I must love and live" (292). Anna, nevertheless, reminds herself that she cannot abandon her son, for without him "there can be no life for me even with the one I love" (292).

Second, soon Anna summons Vronsky to Vrede's garden, where she admits to him she has confessed their affair to her husband. However she is sorely disappointed in Vronsky, whom she now senses is weak, confused, and indecisive. In response, misunderstanding the reason for his stern outward mien as he thinks of the inevitable duel, Anna believes "her last hope has been disappointed. This was not what she had expected" (315). This obstacle, in contrast to the corresponding steeplechase obstacle, is *not* overcome, nor, ominously, will it be later in the sequence.

Sequence 2, motif 3

Anna and Vronsky surmount a societal obstacle, although a hint of danger follows

In this second sequence, the *societal obstacle* motif also is particularly significant.

Anna continues to be drawn to the allure and comfort of Petersburg society. "She felt that the position she enjoyed in society, which had seemed so insignificant to her in the morning, was precious to her, and that she would not be able to exchange it for the shameful position of a woman who has abandoned her husband and son and joined her lover" (293).

Both Anna and Vronsky are tempted to forsake their increasingly complicated love and yield to the persuasive appeals of competing interests: Anna's desire for societal approbation and Vronsky's ambition for career advancement and self-fulfillment.

At Princess Betsy's croquet party, Anna admits to herself that "this whole accustomed social situation was so easy, while what awaited her was so difficult, that for a moment she was undecided whether she might stay" (301).

Meanwhile, initially envious of his accomplished colleague Serpukhovskoy, Vronsky is tempted to indulge his ambition and pursue his career, rather than an increasingly complicated relationship with Anna. But, like Anna, Vronsky soon concludes, "I need nothing, nothing but this happiness" with Anna (313). Both again surmount the societal barrier.

Sequence 2, motif 5

Anna and Vronsky surmount an obstacle in their relationship, although they experience a momentary lack of trust in each other and Vronsky nearly overreacts

In addition to Anna's anguish from the debacle in Vrede's garden, she is further perplexed by the "very dull week" Vronsky spends indulging in base "national pleasures" with a foreign prince whom he is assigned to entertain (353-54). While he is away, she experiences powerful bouts of jealousy. When Vronsky responds to another of her summons and they meet in her home, Anna is acrimonious and accusatory, provoking Vronsky's overreaction: for the moment he regards Anna "as a man looks at a faded flower he has plucked" and destroyed (358).

Anna tells Vronsky that she expects to die in childbirth, and relates her frightening dream of a repugnant French-speaking muzhik, which dream Vronsky silently compares to his own. Shaken, Vronsky claims the dream is nonsense, "aware himself that there was no conviction in his voice" (362). Portentiously, they will *not* fully surmount this obstacle of attenuated love within their relationship until Anna nearly dies in childbirth, and Vronsky realizes how much he does love and need her.

Sequence 2, motif 4

Anna and Vronsky surmount a family obstacle; the family continues pursuit

In sequence 2, motif 4 now occurs a second time. Angered that Anna has received Vronsky in his home against his explicit demands, Karenin, "with resolution and firmness," confiscates incriminating letters written by Vronsky to Anna. She remonstrates to her husband that "it is not even respectable to hit someone who is down" (364), a faint echo of Vronsky's kicking Frou-Frou after breaking her back by his awkward movement. Again, Karenin's fury and this family obstacle are only assuaged at Anna's deathbed.

Sequence 2, motif 6

Having surmounted many difficult obstacles, Anna and Vronsky fail just as success seems assured; Vronsky, self-absorbed, makes an awkward movement and Anna perishes; again Vronsky appears inept and bewildered

In this sequence, motif 6 again closely parallels the steeplechase. One might expect that, having given birth to her and Vronsky's daughter, Anna and her lover could feel celebratory, but that opportunity is denied them as Anna contracts a life-threatening infection. When Karenin arrives as Anna appears to be dying, he sees Vronsky, "his face buried in his hands, weeping." Reminiscent of a jockey at the steeplechase, Vronsky, sitting with "his back to the side of the low chair," sees Karenin and jumps up, but then "sat down again, drawing his head down between his shoulders as if he wished to disappear" (411). Vronsky appears to have repeated his steeplechase's awkward "sitting down" movement and subsequent despair.

Anna now pleads for Karenin's forgiveness. Vronsky again puts his hands to his face. Anna orders Vronsky to remove them and look at Karenin, whom she praises as a saint (413). As at the steeplechase, Karenin has overtaken the fallen Vronsky.

Later, Karenin tells Vronsky he has forgiven Anna, and he "pray[s] to God that He not take from me the happiness of forgiveness!" (414). Once more recalling a jockey's stance while feeling humiliated and defeated, Vronsky, "in a stooping, unstraightened posture looked at [Karenin] from under his brows" (414). As at the conclusion of the steeplechase, Karenin has won; Vronsky is vanquished.

Soon, "shamed, humiliated, guilty" (415), Vronsky concludes he can escape his ignominy only through suicide (417). As he shoots himself in the chest, barely missing his heart, he "staggered and sat down on the floor, looking around himself in surprise" (418), his confusion and ineptness once more echoing the steeplechase disgrace.

Sequence 3, motif 1

Anna initially is agitated and hesitant; Vronsky appears inept and bewildered

Karenin recognizes that Anna continues to love Vronsky and reluctantly agrees to a divorce, and even to relinquishing his son to Anna.

Upon hearing from Princess Betsy of Karenin's concessions and that Anna would receive him, Vronsky rushes to Anna's bedside: "His passion seized her. . . . His feeling communicated itself to her."

For a long time, Anna, now uncertain and hesitant, is unable to speak to Vronsky. Then she responds: "'Yes, you possess me and I am yours,' she finally got out" (434).

Vronsky urges her to go with him to Europe. Anna vacillates momentarily, concerned about what that might mean for Seryozha, but then agrees.

Betraying an obtuse self-absorption and emotional ineptness, Vronsky "simply could not understand how, at this moment of their reunion, she could think about her son, about divorce."

When Vronsky attempts to redirect her attention from her husband and son to himself, Anna again expresses her painful ambivalence: "Ah, why didn't I die? It would have been better!" (435).

Sequence 3, motif 2

Anna deftly deflects blame and rationalizes her guilt;
Vronsky regains composure

Upon Anna's recovery from her illness, she and Vronsky flee with baby Annie, but without Seryozha, to Europe, traveling for three months and then settling in a small Italian town.

There Vronsky meets Golenishchev, a former comrade from the Corps of Pages, who, seeing Anna, is "struck by her beauty and still more by the simplicity with which she accepted her situation."

Anna makes no attempt to conceal her relations with Vronsky. She candidly tells Golenishchev that she and Vronsky are "moving together to a new rented house, known locally as a palazzo" (461), and then wonders whether she has behaved as Vronsky would wish. But Vronsky admires her sincerity, simplicity, and directness, and casts her "a long, tender look" (462). Again it appears that Anna has deflected blame from herself and her lover.

In Italy, Anna feels herself "unpardonably happy and filled with the joy of life" (463). However, rationalizing her guilty pleasures, she tries to convince herself that she really is miserable with the comforting lie that "I, too, suffer and will suffer. . . . I did a bad thing and therefore I do not want happiness" (464).

Sequence 3, motif 3

Anna and Vronsky surmount a societal obstacle, although
a hint of danger follows

By settling in Italy, Anna and Vronsky obviate the need to confront Russian society. Similarly, on Vronsky's country estate societal challenges are minimal. However, during the two weeks he and Anna spend in St. Petersburg when Anna briefly visits her son, society presents a serious challenge. Here society is open to Vronsky, but closed to Anna. Even Anna's presumed friends, Princess Betsy and Vronsky's formerly sympathetic sister-in-law Varya, are reluctant to be seen with her (529). For the most part, Anna disregards society's painful rebuffs, including Lydia Ivanovna's cruel and humiliating refusals to allow a meeting with Seryozha. Attempting to disregard society, Anna redirects her focus to her son.

Sequence 3, motif 4

Anna and Vronsky surmount a family obstacle; the family continues pursuit

For Anna, "even the separation from her son, whom she loved, did not torment her at first . . . the more she knew of Vronsky, the more she loved him," although, ominously, she "sought and failed to find anything not beautiful in him" for the time being (464). But a year later her resurgent love for Seryozha culminates in the emotionally wrenching visit of mother and son on Seryozha's birthday.

Anna "had never expected that seeing him would have so strong an effect on her" (537). She is far from overcoming this family obstacle threatening her love for Vronsky. By contrast, when Anna accidentally sees Karenin, she feels loathing, spite, and envy, not regret.

Subsequently, Anna's sorrow at being separated from her son is portrayed through the aforementioned metonym as she utilizes a photograph of Vronsky to push Seryozha's picture out of an album, much as Vronsky's presence has done to Seryozha in real life. Clearly, in full contrast to the steeplechase, neither has this part of the family obstacle been surmounted.

Sequence 3, motif 5

Anna and Vronsky surmount an obstacle in their relationship, although they experience a momentary lack of trust in each other and Vronsky nearly overreacts

This motif and the following, motif 6, will have great significance for Anna and Vronsky in this third sequence, and again in sequence 4. Although Anna and Vronsky will overcome their mutual anger and leave St. Petersburg for the country reconciled, they first must surmount a terribly difficult obstacle: in defiance of Vronsky's expressed wishes, Anna insists on attending a St. Petersburg opera, thereby issuing a defiant challenge to society — and to Vronsky. He speaks to Anna with sharpness (542), as had Karenin after the steeplechase scene (212), and Anna again feigns bafflement at his agitation. Finally, "with tenderness in his voice, but with coldness in his eyes" Vronsky implores her not to go. Nonetheless, Anna remains adamant. Vronsky experiences "for the first time a feeling of vexation, almost of anger, with Anna for her deliberate refusal to comprehend her position" (543). Portentously, neither is this obstacle overcome.

Sequence 3, motif 6

After having surmounted many difficult obstacles, Anna and Vronsky fail just as success seems assured; Vronsky, self-absorbed, makes an awkward movement and Anna perishes; Vronsky again is inept and bewildered

While at the opera, Anna flaunts her unconventionality before Petersburg society. Vronsky initially remains at the hotel. He is vexed at her behavior, yet feels chagrined at not having accompanied her. "'What about me? Am I afraid or did I pass it on to Tushkevich to chaperone her? However you look at it, it's stupid, stupid. . . . And why does she put me in such a position?' he said, waving his arm." There follows a small scene that Tolstoy adds very late in the writing process (second-half of 1876; variant 146, ms. 90) which appears to be another partial replay of Vronsky's awkward movement and anger at his fallen mount at the end of the steeplechase: "In that movement he brushed against the little table on which the seltzer water and decanter of cognac stood and almost knocked it over. He went to catch it, dropped it, kicked the table in vexation, and rang the bell" (544).

When Vronsky does arrive at the opera he, perplexed, "felt he must do something, but did not know what." Anna underscores her dissatisfaction with Vronsky as she sarcastically remarks to him, "You got here late and missed the best aria" [solo performance] (548). The audience also hisses Vronsky as early in the next act he leaves to find Anna. She greets him at the hotel with the reproach, "You, you're to blame for it all" (549), hurling the very accusation Frou-Frou, had she been able much earlier, might have directed at him. However, while Frou-Frou's claims would have been entirely justified, Anna's are only partly so. She bears much responsibility for her tormenting loss of Seryozha, with whom she and Vronsky perhaps could have left Russia but for Anna's gratuitous refusal to accept Karenin's magnanimity,[2] and for her societal humiliation, for it was she who, despite Vronsky's pleas, insisted on attending the opera.

Figuratively, Anna suffers a double mortification (death) at the clear realization of the complete loss of all hope for regaining her son *and* former position in society. In her mind, however, Vronsky bears by far the greater part of the blame for her suffering, and he, again, appears confused and inept.

---

[2] Gary Saul Morson persuasively argues that Anna declines her husband's magnanimity since "his very goodness offends her, in part, because it deprives her of her earlier excuses for mistreating him" (Poetic Justice 190).

Sequence 4, motif 1

Anna initially is agitated and hesitant; Vronsky appears inept and bewildered

When Dolly visits Anna at Vronsky's country estate, Anna gives the impression of being entirely secure, contented, and confident, as though finally living the fantasy which arose in her mind as she read the English novel on the train following the reconciliation of the Oblonskys. However, Anna's deep agitation and anxiety soon become apparent. In their first private conversation, Anna initially insists to Dolly that she is "unforgivably happy." Yet she betrays an underlying uncertainty through her first question: "What's your opinion of my situation? What do you think?" (613).

For his part, Vronsky greets Dolly's arrival while "riding a dark bay thoroughbred, obviously excited from galloping. He worked the reins, trying to hold it back" (610). The scene reminds the reader of Vronsky entering Frou-Frou's stall and seeing "a dark bay horse, shifting her feet on the fresh straw . . . she possessed in the highest degree a quality that made one forget all shortcomings; this quality was *blood*, that blood which *tells*, as the English say" (181-82). Then Vronsky was unable to calm his horse, as he now struggles to rein it in.

Sequence 4, motif 2

Anna deftly deflects blame and rationalizes her guilt; Vronsky regains composure

At Vronsky's country estate, Dolly admires his meticulous and extensive agricultural enterprise and mansion. On the surface, all appears idyllic. Clearly, however, Anna still is troubled by a burden of guilt, beginning with luring Vronsky from Kitty at the Petersburg ball. Yet again she is adept at rationalizing this guilt and deflecting blame from her: "But it wasn't my fault. And whose fault was it? What does 'fault' mean? Could it have been otherwise?" (635). Recalling his much earlier response to Anna's oblique prompting to assist the widow of the railroad workman run over by a train, a composed Vronsky now proudly shows Dolly his new hospital, built largely, it appears, in response to Anna's reproach of him for his stinginess (614).

Sequence 4, motif 3

Anna and Vronsky surmount a societal obstacle, although a hint of danger follows

In the country, Anna experiences very little social life. Only Vronsky participates fully in society. As Anna irritably remarks, "Alexei's been here six months and he's already a member of five or six social institutions — he's a trustee, a judge, a councilor, a juror, and something to do with horses" (633). Anna's social isolation will continue here and in Moscow until her death. Anna is denied her status in society. This obstacle, too, remains insurmountable.

Sequence 4, motif 4

Anna and Vronsky surmount a family obstacle; family continues pursuit

With Dolly visiting her in the country, Anna yearns to lessen the tormenting complexities of her family life. Her deepest anxiety, about which both Anna and Vronsky privately speak with Dolly, cannot be resolved. Anna acknowledges she loves two people with all her heart, Seryozha and Vronsky, "and the one excludes the other. I can't unite them, yet I need only that. And if there isn't that, the rest makes no difference" (640). Vronsky, too, seems happily engaged in much significant activity, but his overriding concern also relates to the family issue. Above all, he desires to find a way to convince Anna she must attempt to obtain a divorce, thus enabling him to legalize their marriage and their children's status. Again, in this last sequence, the family obstacle remains a tormenting, unresolved issue.

Sequence 4, motif 5

Anna and Vronsky surmount an obstacle in their relationship, although they experience a momentary lack of trust in each other and Vronsky nearly overreacts

In the final sequence, again motifs 5 and 6 are particularly revealing. After six relatively happy months in the country, Anna and Vronsky face a difficult challenge as Vronsky gradually reasserts his "male independence" (645), seen most clearly as he attends the October nobility elections. The "cold, stern look he gave [Anna] when he came to announce that he was leaving offended her," causing her to complain that "he has all the rights and I have none" (665-66). When Anna writes to Vronsky on the pretext of Annie's illness and pleads for him to return home immediately, Vronsky is displeased. He tells Anna she must recognize that he has responsibilities. Anna venomously reminds him of neglecting his "responsibilities to go to a concert" (668), undoubtedly referring to his failure to accompany her to the Petersburg opera, allowing her to be subjected to insult.

Anna then demands to be allowed to go with Vronsky to Moscow, to which he responds, "'It's as though you are threatening me. Yet there's nothing I wish more than not to be separated from you,' Vronsky said smiling. But the look that flashed in his eyes as he spoke those tender words was not only the cold, angry look of a persecuted and embittered man." That look forebodes much more — a complete rupture. As Vronsky blurts out: "If it's like this, it is a disaster!" (668).

In Moscow, Vronsky again asserts his freedom as Anna interrogates him about why he stayed with Yashvin at the races since Vronsky could not prevent him from gambling away his money. Vronsky responds with anger: "the main thing is that I wanted to stay and so I did" (705). Anna divulges that she is close to a personal disaster and needs Vronsky near her. He accedes, but "there had settled between them an evil spirit of some sort of struggle, which she could not drive out of his heart and still less out of her own" (707).

Anna continues her descent into a vile, spiteful jealousy, searching for an object to which she might direct her wrath. Soon she settles briefly on Princess Sorokin. For his part, Vronsky gratuitously terms "unnatural" Anna's caring for her ward, Hannah (741). In an ensuing argument, Vronsky threatens her: "This is becoming unbearable! . . . Why do you try my patience? . . . It does have limits" (744). Regardless, and although their relationship remains fragile, Vronsky and Anna relent and experience a momentary, passionate reconciliation before the story's dénouement.

Sequence 4, motif 6

After having surmounted many difficult obstacles, Anna and Vronsky fail just as success seems assured; Vronsky, self-absorbed, makes an awkward movement and Anna perishes; again Vronsky appears inept and bewildered

At the time of Anna's approaching suicide, Vronsky again makes a series of seriously awkward movements, quite plainly recalling those of the steeplechase. In the first place, he misses an opportunity to ameliorate harsh words spoken to Anna. As he is leaving the room, "he saw her face in the mirror, pale, with trembling lips. He would have liked to stop and say something comforting to her, but his legs carried him out of the room before he could think of what to say" (750).

Second, Anna subsequently does her part by approaching Vronsky and standing "silently in the middle of the room, gazing fixedly at him." She has come her half of the way. Vronsky glances at her, frowns briefly, and continues reading a letter. Anna slowly leaves the room. "He could still bring her back, but she reached the door, he remained silent, and only the rustle of the turning page was heard." Belatedly, awkwardly, Vronsky complains that "this is becoming unbearable." Anna responds angrily with the final words she will ever speak to him: "You will regret that," and leaves the room. "Frightened by the desperate look with which these words were spoken, he jumped up and was about to run after her, but, recollecting himself, *sat down again,* clenched his teeth tightly and frowned. This improper — as he found it — threat of something irritated him" (753; emphasis added). As at the steeplechase, Vronsky again *sits down at precisely the wrong time.* In effect he dashes Anna's hopes and breaks her spirit.

At this moment the *two clusters of allegory and symbol* merge.

From the *steeplechase allegorical cluster* one recalls Vronsky's awkward movements: Vronsky "had made a wrong, an unforgivable movement as he lowered himself into the saddle" (199) and breaks Frou-Frou's back. Now, during Anna and Vronsky's last meeting before her suicide, at the same time that Vronsky "sat down again," the novel's only richly elaborated symbol associated with the *train symbolic cluster* also finds expression. As discussed above, this occurs at the moment Vronsky decides his only alternative is to "pay no attention" to Anna, the very thing Anna feels to be so repugnant in the behavior of the repulsive, French-speaking muzhik who, most terrible of all, "paid no attention to her" while "doing his dreadful thing with iron [в железе 9.752] over her" (752).

Now Anna feels she has "never hated anyone as I do this man [Vronsky]!" (761). In her relationship with Vronsky the "zest is gone" and Anna, tellingly, admits, "I no longer have the same savour for him" (763). In one last repetition of his failure to keep pace with Anna, Vronsky writes "in careless hand" that he will return to her only at 10 p.m., as earlier stated, a final reminder to Anna that he will no longer accommodate her if doing so inconveniences him. To Anna, suicide seems her only recourse: "I'll punish him and be rid of everybody and of myself" (768).

Vronsky certainly has failed multiple times to keep pace with Anna. He has squandered several opportunities to overcome quite easily what are, finally, minor obstacles. In the end, to a considerable degree he bears responsibility for breaking Anna's "back," as he did Frou-Frou's. Yet in the final analysis, Anna shares fully in the responsibility for her demise. Unlike Frou-Frou, Anna, too, has made numerous miscalculations concerning relations toward husband, son, lover, and position in society. The burdens of her indulged weaknesses and of her own misjudgments also prove too heavy for her to bear. Death promises the only path to a resolution and release.

The three "deaths" at the end of each preceding sequence — Anna as murder victim after her and Vronsky's first sexual union, the near-death at the time of Annie's birth, and the "death" of Anna's spirit both upon embracing and then for a second time abandoning Seryozha, and upon her mortification from the cruelty of a pretentious society lady at the opera — now culminate in Anna's actual death on the *iron* rails under a massive train.

An important question arises concerning whether Tolstoy *intentionally repeats* this steeplechase pattern of six allegorical motifs in the four sequences, or whether what occurs throughout the novel is mainly *coincidental and random*. Again, I employ the *principle of reasonable probability*. If the most obvious repetitions of motif 6 — Vronsky's awkward movements wholly or in part causing Frou-Frou and Anna's deaths — are intentional, not coincidental, then it seems reasonable to consider the possibility that other steeplechase motifs may be similarly meaningful. Although it has been possible to uncover evidence in support of the six motifs in all four sequences, certain of the repetitions clearly are more obvious, encompassing, and persuasive than others.

Yet I am inclined to believe that Tolstoy had these motifs in mind, although perhaps in the form of an *intuitive* but insistent inner logic, a pattern he sensed recurs in virtually every adulterous love affair. Here his syllogism applies directly to a woman, a mother, who, over time, tires of her unfulfilling husband and becomes unfaithful to him. Anna admits that Karenin is "a good man, truthful, kind and remarkable in his sphere" (112), but emotionally and physically inadequate for her as a woman. The subsequent logical progression proceeds along a generally descending curve of initial hesitancy and agitation; early denial of blame and rationalization of guilt; overcoming significant obstacles to her illicit behavior from society, family, and her new relationship; and, finally, a tragic conclusion when relatively insignificant hurdles appear and irrationally, needlessly acquire huge prominence, resulting in her "death" and ending all relationships.

Over his career, Tolstoy demonstrates a fondness for absolute formulations (e.g., "*All* happy families are alike; *each* unhappy family is unhappy in its own way." [1; emphasis added]). In *Anna Karenina* the author conceives and illustrates, but does not state explicitly, an especially elaborate form of one such centrally important but unspoken assertion: "An adulterous relationship eventually culminates in tragedy for all — spouse, children, lover, and self." Among many other messages in *Anna Karenina*, this one is particularly insistent and compelling. What makes Tolstoy's achievement in this novel so remarkable is that the fullest sustained expression of this deeply felt belief is, for Tolstoy, unusually unobtrusive and subtly embedded in the structure of the four sequences. The sequences implicitly link to recurring allegorical motifs from the steeplechase. These motifs reverberate, continually reinforcing an indirect but powerful message.

Another significant question remains. Is the reader generally aware of the repeating sequences and of the allegorical motifs developing within them? No, as a rule, I think not. However, upon subsequent readings, the more thoughtful, careful reader at least senses a partial patterning without ever needing to articulate it. Though indirectly expressed, this patterning may work, as does an archetype, on the readers' subconscious and draw them to important insights and conclusions in a manner that can be far more impressive and memorable than are explicitly expressed teachings, such as those in Tolstoy's last important novel, *Resurrection*.

To illustrate further, each sequence contains an additional important embedded structural feature. Each sequence begins with an opportunity for Anna, were she to make increasingly difficult choices, to recalibrate her moral and ethical coordinates and start over with a more or less clean slate. And, as we have seen, each sequence ends with her "death" — twice figuratively, once nearly, and the last, literally. Even if only subliminally, this trajectory of marital infidelity feels ineluctable and tragic as, surely, Tolstoy wishes his readers to infer and remember.

Specifically, the *first sequence* begins as Anna travels to Moscow to visit the estranged Oblonskys. As the reader learns subsequently, Anna had been reluctant to leave her essentially well-ordered and stable life in St. Petersburg (97).

Her story begins with a clean slate. In Moscow, however, she meets and is quickly drawn to Vronsky. Although on her train trip back to St. Petersburg she insists to herself that she feels "firm and irreproachable," and defends her husband as being "a good man, truthful, kind, and remarkable in his own sphere" (112), in her heart she is only a few beats away from yielding to Vronsky's romantic appeal. This first sequence ends following her first sexual intimacy with Vronskay with an allusion to Anna as a murder victim. Additionally, the sequence chronicles the "death" of Anna's moral self, a fatal impairment of her conscience, and a serious blow to her self-esteem.

The *second sequence* begins as Anna implies that Vronsky is essentially correct when he asserts that, feeling duplicitous, she is suffering over everything that is most important to her: "over society, and your son, and your husband." Although Anna claims she is not anguishing over her husband, when she acknowledges to herself that she has deceived him, "tears of shame welled up in her eyes" (188). Had she resolutely wished to do so, at this point she could have taken up a clean slate and begun over. But her passion for Vronsky prevented such a difficult turnabout. The sequence ends with the scene of Anna's near-death at the birth of Annie. For her, this sequence also includes an emphasis on the "death" of Karenin, her contrite and repentant, legal husband.

In reality, the *third sequence* begins as Anna apparently experiences a few moments of mental and emotional clarity during her delirium just prior to her postpartum near-death. She tells Karenin that another person within her fell in love with Vronsky and wanted to hate her husband, but "Now I'm real, I'm whole" (412). Again, a potential turning point arises. Yet as her health improves, Anna again yields to Vronsky's appeal, declaring "Yes, you possess me and I am yours" (434). They soon escape to Italy and there begin a new life together. This sequence ends with Anna "dying" twice as she abandons Seryozha a second and final time and is mortified by the insult she receives at the opera. Sequence 3 shows that Anna has irreparably suffered the loss, or "deaths," of her son Seryozha and of her respectable position in society.

The *fourth sequence* begins as Anna reflects on her heart-rending birthday visit to Seryozha. She admits that she "had never expected that seeing him would have so strong an effect on her" (537). This could have been a catalyst for turning her life around, but, owing to her feelings of loathing, spite, and envy when Karenin entered Seryozha's room (537), Anna chooses instead to flee again with Vronsky, this time to his country estate. This sequence ends with Anna's tragic suicide. Finally, after so many deaths in other sequences, Anna's own physical annihilation occurs. In the four sequences she also has chosen to relinquish her moral conscience and integrity, Karenin, Seryozha, her standing in society, and, now in sequence 4, most devastating of all, even Vronsky, for whom she has sacrificed everything she once considered to be her sources of peace of mind and personal happiness.

Chapter 5

COMPARISON OF EARLY AND FINAL DRAFTS CONTAINING THE STEEPLECHASE ALLEGORY AND THE MUZHIK SYMBOL

Having considered the major clusters of symbols and allegories arising from Anna's Moscow to St. Petersburg train ride and the subsequent muzhik nightmares and from Vronsky's steeplechase as they all appear in the completed *Anna Karenina* (January 1878), I will briefly compare the two earliest fragmentary drafts of the novel (March and April 1873)[1] with the completed text. The purpose of the comparison is to demonstrate that Tolstoy intended to utilize the steeplechase allegory and the muzhik symbol from the very earliest drafts, thus indicating a primary importance of these elements in the novel.

The often sketchy conception and development of the March 1873 version includes 12 segments entitled "chapters," some of which are only a few words long. The most detailed chapters portray the steeplechase.

The first draft's chapter 2 (408-09) follows a depiction of an evening in a high society salon and takes place on the day of the steeplechase. Chapter 2 is significant primarily because it contains the information that Tatiana Stavrovich (Anna), after six years of marriage, finally is expecting her *first* child, of whom Balashov (Vronsky), not her husband Mikhail Stavrovich (Karenin), is the father-to-be. Beginning with chapter 3 and continuing through the first part of chapter 6,

---

[1] For the most accurate formulation of the two earliest drafts, see Zhdanov, «K istorii» (397-442). This is the source I will use for the two drafts quoted in this chapter.

filling approximately ten of the first draft's 23 printed pages, Tolstoy provides information directly connected to the steeplechase. Clearly, from the earliest draft, the steeplechase is central to Tolstoy's artistic vision and form in *Anna Karenina*.

Tolstoy's choice for the name of Balashov's mount is "Dzhim," written in Russian [Джим]. At some point as the author rereads this draft, he crosses Dzhim out and substitutes "Tiny," given in English. Following Balashov's visit to Tatiana (whom Balashov addresses not as Tatiana, but as Tania) and from just prior to the race, the horse now consistently bears the name "Tani" in Russian [Тани], an indeclinable form very close to Tania [Таня]. Most likely, Tolstoy regarded the names Tania and Tani as *too* blatantly parallel, later replacing them with Anna and Frou-Frou.

Balashov (Vronsky) considers his "most dangerous rival" in the race to be Miliutin[2] (later, Makhotin). Note Miliutin's detailed description, virtually all of which is deleted from the later, more allegorical portrayal of Makhotin/Seryozha. Miliutin is a small, thin, young military staff-captain weighing 115 pounds, compared to Balashov's 157. Miliutin has weak, sugary eyes and is from highest society. An excellent rider, Miliutin is an arrogant intellectual snob. He espouses the faddish liberalism of his day. He also laughs loudly in an unnatural, affected manner, while "displaying his long teeth" (413). Obviously, to this point, Miliutin shares no characteristic with the later Makhotin/Seryozha, other than the long teeth. Although Tani the horse already clearly parallels Tania, as later will the allegorical Frou-Frou parallel Anna, Miliutin and his horse Nel'son have no apparent affiliation with characters in the first draft or final version of the novel. For one thing, Tania's first child has not yet been born and could not play

---

[2] For a picture of the real-life A.D. Miliutin, see Cruise, 5.

a figurative role in the steeplechase, as will Makhotin/Seryozha later. Only subsequently will Tolstoy expand the allegory of the steeplechase to include Seryozha and Karenin as Makhotin and Gladiator, respectively.

Both the first and final drafts portray Balashov riding an agitated, reluctant mount that tugs against her reins, bouncing her rider and trying to delude (*обмануть*) him. In both this and the final text, two other riders, Miliutin on Nel'son and an unnamed Cossack officer and horse, sprint ahead of Balashov/Vronsky as the race begins. In the completed novel, Makhotin on Gladiator and Kuzovlev riding Diana set the early pace. Contrasting with the allegorical pair Tani/Tania, Miliutin, his mount Nel'son, and the Cossack officer appear to be meager, faintly realistic portrayals devoid of any allegorical weight. On the other hand, in the final text it seems clear that all the named participants in the steeplechase — Frou-Frou, Makhotin, Gladiator, and possibly even Diana and Kuzovlev — have acquired additional allegorical stature.

At this point in the final version, Tolstoy includes a steeplechase barrier missing from draft one. Frou-Frou leaps over an obstacle not far behind the horses Gladiator and Diana. Vronsky and Frou-Frou nearly land on the fallen Diana and her rider Kuzovlev. But Frou-Frou makes a powerful and adroit movement, and clears Diana. As mentioned, the author here and throughout the race emphasizes Frou-Frou's agility and strength. On an allegorical level, Anna demonstrates her adroitness in avoiding society's muddy, banal, emotionally slippery debauchery. Thereby, she averts blame through rationalizing her guilt of illicit behavior. She and Vronsky justify their liaison as being more than mere promiscuity. True love must reflect a deeply serious, sincere, and enduring commitment, and, as they have convinced themselves, their love is genuine, unlike that of Princess Betsy and Tushkevich/Diana and Kuzovlev, who wallow in the filth of their shallow immorality. This barrier, then, represents an important addition, establishing the difference between trivial societal indulgence and what Anna and Vronsky consider their deep and sincere love, generally misunderstood by others.

At the second obstacle (the first in draft one [(414)], Tani leaps *slightly late* from a point too near the barrier and knocks it with a hind leg. Leaping this barrier appears to have no meaning beyond the realistic portrayal of a race in which the horse makes but overcomes a slight miscalculation. In the final draft, this second obstacle is identified as the "Devil" and stands directly in front of the tsar's pavilion filled with members of *high society*. Surmounting this barrier appears to correlate with overcoming the challenges society presents to the Anna/Vronsky relationship. Frou-Frou clears the boards "without the least change of movement . . . the boards vanished, and [Vronsky] only heard something knock behind him. Excited by Gladiator going ahead of her, the horse had risen *too early* before the barrier and knocked against it with a back hoof. But her pace did not change" (198; emphasis added), and Vronsky is hit in the face with a lump of mud kicked up by Gladiator. Frou-Frou's early launch not only seems more realistic, but also relates to Anna's premature and mistaken dismissal of society's powerful appeal for her; the knock, to an ominous presage of society's future resurgent appeal; and mud, to the societal disgrace Vronsky must bear for his disreputable behavior in relation to Karenin and for his own disregard of societal expectations, however unjust and pretentious they may be.

Draft one's next obstacle is a river. Balashov senses reservation in Tani and draws his legs more tightly into her sides, clicking his tongue in encouragement. But Tani, instantaneously divining his meaning and replying in thought, assures herself, "No, I am not afraid." She leaps into the water, struggles briefly, but soon rises "from the slime" and clambers up onto dry ground. At this point Miliutin is just behind and gaining on Balashov. When Balashov glances back, he sees Miliutin "smile unnaturally" (414).

In both drafts, Balashov/Vronsky and their mounts recognize when it is time to distance themselves from their competitors. As Balashov urges his horse on faster, Tani, sounding very much like Tania might, says to herself, "So I need to give more. Oh, I can give much more" (415), and she pulls away from Miliutin, although he continues in close pursuit. Later, similar to Tani, "Frou-Frou, already knowing [Vronsky's] thoughts, speeded up noticeably without any urging," but is blocked from taking an inside position. As Vronsky now thinks of passing on the outside, "Frou-Frou switched step and started to go ahead precisely that way." Vronsky works the reins, urging Frou-Frou on, and after taking several strides together with Gladiator, moves ahead on the slope. Still, Vronsky can feel Gladiator close behind him "and constantly heard just at his back the steady tread and the short, still quite fresh breathing of Gladiator's nostrils" (198). In this final version, Tolstoy shows Frou-Frou's oneness with her rider, both in her sensitivity to his desires and, when required, in her willingness to distance herself from Makhotin/Seryozha. In the first draft, since Tania has no Seryozha-like child, Miliutin does not need to correspond to anyone in physical traits. Hence, as we have seen, the author feels free to portray him in considerable detail, solely as an actual person in the race, without an allegorical overlay.

At the following, most difficult barrier (a wall and a ditch), many of Balashov's society friends stand waiting (415). Now Balashov and Tani are one in movement and confidence. Tani leaps at the precise moment required, clears the barrier, and speeds onward without breaking stride. In the final text, a confident Vronsky and Frou-Frou surmount the Irish bank, "the most difficult" obstacle (allegorically, a threat within their own relationship). But first *both* horse and rider experience a moment's lack of confidence in the other. Vronsky even "raised his whip, but felt at once that his doubt was groundless" (198-99). In the completed text this crisis of confidence, as in the Anna/Vronsky relationship, occurs late in the steeplechase and appears to be the final challenge before the disastrous ending of their race for happiness in an illicit affair.

In the first version of the novel, only a relatively trifling barrier now remains (415-16), a four-and-a-half-foot-wide ditch with water. At this barrier Tat'iana Stavrovich, the horse Tani's alter ego, awaits Balashov and Tani's approach. Tolstoy here informs the reader without elaboration that Tania has had a *dream*, presumably linked to the steeplechase, foretelling a catastrophe. In the final version, the portentous muzhik dream occurs later, apart from the race and is connected to the train ride cluster of symbols, not the steeplechase.

Balashov catches sight of Tania and urges Tani on. Tani leaps slightly early and thus must clear not four-and-a-half but seven feet, yet she is fully confident of success. Neither horse nor rider feels apprehensive about this minor irregularity. *Both* focus only on racing beyond the barrier to the finish line and awaiting glory.

Suddenly, horse and rider are jolted. Upon landing, one of Tani's rear hooves sinks into the soft ditch bank and her hindquarters collapse. Owing to *her* awkward movement (leaping too early), Tani breaks her back. Miliutin "with his white teeth" (38; Vronsky's trait in the final version) dashes by and wins the race, followed by the always anonymous, nearly invisible Cossack officer. Balashov, "in a frenzy, kicks his heel into his horse's side" (38) and then winces when a doctor touches his side while helping him into a carriage. The reader infers that Balashov is slightly hurt, while Tani lies mortally injured.

Thus, in this first draft, Tani is essentially responsible for her own demise and even for causing injury to Balashov. Her poor timing, overestimation of her ability, and awkwardness cause her ruin. This race reflects the author's earlier intentions of portraying Tania as clearly the more guilty party in the relationship.

In the final version, a self-absorbed, vain, and arrogant Vronsky urges Frou-Frou on in order to vanquish all competitors and secure for himself a glorious victory. Vronsky's attitude and aspiration relate to his ambition and pride, later impelling him to groom an extravagant country estate and, as soon as possible, stand for office in nobility elections.

Frou-Frou sails over the ditch without difficulty, but Vronsky's awkward movement in sitting down in his saddle at precisely the wrong moment (there is not a hint of this "sitting down" awkwardness in the first draft) breaks Frou-Frou's back. Here the reader feels compassion for the victim Frou-Frou and disgust at the inept, careless Vronsky. Tolstoy has reversed their roles. Now it is Vronsky who bears *all* the blame for Frou-Frou's demise. The author can allow himself this black-and-white steeplechase portrait because he introduces Anna's substantial share of the blame in a symbolic depiction of her train ride from Moscow to St. Petersburg after reuniting Dolly and Stiva Oblonsky, and in the developing muzhik symbol, first encountered in the train ride at the Bologovo station. Therefore, the final race can specifically focus on Vronsky's failures.

To emphasize, *with the exception of Tani and Tania*, characters in the first draft's steeplechase do not serve as allegories for characters outside of the steeplechase, whereas they do in significant ways throughout the finished novel.

To indicate the direction of Tolstoy's early thinking about *Anna Karenina* and to conclude an overview of the first draft of the novel, I will sketch brief highlights of the remaining chapters in draft one (417-23). The following chapter, chapter 6, contains a discussion between Tania and her husband Mikhail Stavrovich, during which Tania *denies* any infidelity with Balashov. In the final version, Anna confesses everything to her husband after the steeplechase. In draft one, on the following day, Tania's spiritually devout *sister* Kitty informs Mikhail that, indeed, Tania is unfaithful and that society is aware of her behavior. Mikhail leaves St. Petersburg.

Chapters 7 through 10 consist only of a few words each. They project the continuation of the novel to cover the period of Tania's pregnancy and the birth of her *first* child, sired by Balashov. Chapter 11 briefly outlines Mikhail Stavrovich's Christian forgiveness and granting of a divorce to Tania.

Chapter 12, the concluding chapter in the first draft, is barely over two pages long and portrays Balashov, now in retirement from the military, at loose ends. For her part, Tania has become irrationally jealous. Their now *two* children live isolated from close relatives. All that remains to Tania and Balashov are "animal passions and a life of luxury" (422). Tania admits to herself that she has destroyed the lives of two "kind and good men," and, in despair, resorts to suicide. Initially, Tolstoy's heroine ends her life by drowning in the Neva River. In revising the draft, the author crosses out the drowning death and has Tania perish "on the rails" (423), thus already presaging the pervasive iron imagery in the final novel.

A month after completing the first partial draft in March 1873, Tolstoy produces a second, briefer text (15 printed pages [423-42, including facsimiles]) compared to 18 in draft one [404-23]). But the second draft is more comprehensive.[3]

---

[3] In the Jubilee Edition (Tolstoy, L.N., *Polnoe sobranie*), the first draft (t. 20:23-46) is mistakenly listed second, and the second, more

While the muzhik nightmares appear prominently in this April 1873 draft, Anna's train ride from Moscow back to her family in St. Petersburg makes its appearance in the written text only sometime after the beginning of 1874.[4]

Draft two again begins with a salon gathering and a gossipy discussion of the distinctly unattractive Nana Karenina and her wrinkly husband Aleksei Karenin, which conversation ends as the Karenins arrive. Gagin (to become Vronsky in later drafts), a short, stocky officer with a ring in one ear, also soon makes an appearance. Nana playfully fingers a *penknife* and a string of black pearls, which she coquettishly draws across her teeth (430). Nana and Gagin retreat to a corner and all, including Karenin, observe their intimate tête-à-tête, at the conclusion of which Nana privately declares her love to Gagin. Later that night, Karenin confronts his wife with her obvious indiscretions and dangerous intent, but she denies any culpability.

For the purposes of this study, what is most important in the April 1873 draft appears next in a meeting months later between Nana (Anna), now pregnant, and her child's father-to-be, Gagin (Vronsky). Now the author introduces the centrally important *muzhik dreams*. Gagin comes to visit Nana after having had too much to drink with comrades and dreaming of a repulsive, French-speaking muzhik. There is no reference to the completed novel's muzhik who tracked bears for Vronsky. At their meeting, Nana confesses to Gagin that she feels guilty for her deception of Karenin, whom she, nonetheless, dismisses as a defenseless sheep who would not

---

comprehensive but briefer draft, first (t. 20:14-23). V.A. Zhdanov effectively argues for the order I follow. See especially Zhdanov, V.A., *Tvorcheskaia istoriia* (7-18).

[4] The train ride section belongs to the seventh redaction. See "Opisanie 195" in Tolstoi, L.N., *Polnoe sobranie* (20:183-90) for a treatment of the difficulty in dating Tolstoy's drafts.

resist were she to cut his throat. Then Nana tells Gagin that she believes her quandary will soon end because she had a dream long ago, which dream, Gagin recognizes, parallels his own. The dreams of Gagin and Nana (436, 442) are *virtually the same* as those of Anna and Vronsky found in the final text. However, these dreams are not developed or even mentioned again in the remainder of the draft.

It is significant that in *Anna Karenina*'s earliest two drafts, Tolstoy had clearly in mind the central core of his two allegorical and symbolic clusters.

On the one hand, the steeplechase occupies a position of great prominence in draft one, as allegorically it will throughout the completed novel. On the other, the repulsive, French-speaking muzhik appears in full form in draft two, written within a month of draft one. In subsequent drafts and revisions, the author develops these linkages further, but their primary concepts and early expressions are essentially in place from the beginning in 1873. Much of what Tolstoy will do in later variants and drafts is to extend and deepen these linkages.

For instance, the early drafts of the novel do not include the Bologovo station's "huddled shadow of a man" slipping under Anna's legs while the sound of "a hammer striking iron" is heard (102). This crouching shadow ultimately will be linked to the muzhik of Anna's nightmare and recur thrice more near the end of the novel. Similarly related, though absent from early drafts, is the scene in which Vronsky leaps up, intending to run after Anna, when she has told him he will regret saying that their relations were becoming unbearable. But then he, "recollecting himself, sat down again" (753). The reader will recognize that at this moment Vronsky has just played *his* final role in the breaking of Anna's back, as he had Frou-Frou's through his unforgivable, clumsy movement at the steeplechase.

Having established the essential allegorical steeplechase and the symbolic muzhik clusters of linkages in the earliest 1873 drafts, Tolstoy will continue to extend, deepen, and polish them until they attain a high level of artistic significance in the completed text of *Anna Karenina.*

CONCLUSION

In the completed *Anna Karenina*, Vronsky and Anna visit the Russian artist Mikhailov, who is also residing in Italy. Vronsky comments on Mikhailov's "amazing mastery" in his picture of Christ before Pilate. The omniscient narrator informs his readers that Vronsky's observation "about technique grated painfully on Mikhailov's heart and, glancing angrily at Vronsky, he suddenly scowled" (474). Mikhailov's visceral response mirrors Tolstoy's often expressed sensitivities. Technique is for labored, mannered, unnatural art, while the artist's aspiration should be to provide a clear, uncluttered expression of sincere and irrepressible feeling.

In Tolstoy's *What is Art?* published in 1898, twenty years after *Anna Karenina*, the author rails at those who presume *to interpret* a work of art:

> 'Critics explain!' What do they explain? The artist, if a real artist, has by his work transmitted to others the feeling he experienced. What is there, then, to explain? If a work is a good work of art, then the feeling expressed by the artist — be it moral or immoral — transmits itself to other people. If it is transmitted to others, then they feel it, and all interpretations are superfluous. (194)

Yet, speaking specifically of *Anna Karenina*, Tolstoy had insisted that his novel's meaning is intertwined within essential linkages, impossible to express directly in words. As noted, he actually invites the critic to "continually lead

Conclusion

readers through the endless *labyrinth of linkages* forming the essence of art, to those laws serving as the basis of these linkages" (Tolstoy, *Polnoe sobranie* 62:268-69; emphasis added). Further, Tolstoy admits that he intentionally has hidden the keystone to his novel among these internal connections (or linkages) and urges, even taunts, the reader and critic to look very carefully "for the keystone and you will find it" (Tolstoy, *Polnoe sobranie* 62:377). Thus Tolstoy invites a consideration of *Anna Karenina*'s sophisticated structure or "architecture," and of other formal, technical aspects, for in them lies embedded the novel's most significant meaning.

In this study, I have examined previously unnoticed or briefly mentioned connections, linkages, and keystones in *Anna Karenina*. I do not presume to have divined all that Tolstoy had in mind as he wrote his novel and the above quoted passages from letters to friends, but I am inclined to believe that the two clusters of symbols and allegories analyzed in this study are prominent among the novel's most important connections, linkages, and keystones that merit consideration.

Anna's significant peasant dreams are linked *symbolically* to a major weakness in her personality: a tendency, first, to exaggerate appealing features of an attractive new acquaintance and then, as time passes and reality inevitably brings layers of disillusionment, to exaggerate the same person's inadequacies. The peasant *symbolized* in her recurring dreams from long before her liaison with Vronsky also *allegorically* reflects a grotesque Karenin, which facilitates the abandonment of her husband. The cycle then begins again as Vronsky by degrees displaces Karenin in her dreams and nightmares, ending in Anna's even greater disillusionment and propelling her toward self-destruction.

Conclusion

It seems apparent that Anna, initially subconsciously, conceives of Karenin and Vronsky as paralleling the repugnant muzhik, mainly because of the inability or unwillingness of her "two husbands" to consistently and nearly exclusively address her emotional and physical needs. In this sphere, the peasant linkage, first glimpsed as an emerging image in Anna's train ride back to Moscow, forms a keystone in the novel's meaning. Anna will sacrifice everything, including that which is of greatest value to her — husband, son, society, lover and even her own life — in her tragic, obsessive quest for more complete emotional and physical fulfillment. When Karenin proves incapable of satisfying her needs, and Vronsky is unable to forego interest in all *but* her, Anna's disenchantment and desperation mount, ultimately finding expression in the revenge and self-annihilation forecast by the muzhik symbol.

It must be emphasized, however, that the muzhik *symbol* goes beyond allegorical/symbolic associations with Karenin and Vronsky. Even in its more allegorical dimension, the muzhik in relation to Anna's 'two husbands' is far more complex and dynamic than is the stable and clearly allegorical relationship of Frou-Frou and Anna. The multifaceted muzhik symbol possesses greater metaphysical and ontological status. The muzhik symbol combines with the loose sheet of iron blown about haphazardly by the fierce, snowy wind at the Bologovo train station to suggest an indefinable, unpredictable, and uncontrollable mortal danger set loose by unknowable, destructive forces. The grotesque, relatively incomprehensible muzhik — like the sheet of iron, the massive train, the train wheels, the railroad rails, and that "huge and implacable" force that "pushed at her head and dragged over her" at the moment of Anna's death (768) — conjures impressions of hostile, gruesome, pursuing forces of compulsion, injury, and death. One seems to become vulnerable to this menacing

Conclusion

power of retribution through grave violation of impersonal, disinterested, imprecise cosmic imperatives. The muzhik progresses along his perplexing metamorphosis in size, shape, feature, function, and significance. The disheveled muzhik is not merely a symbolic image or a "proto-symbol," but a full and robust *symbol*, worthy to stand in the circle of other leading Russian literary symbols.

A comparably pervasive and encompassing set of connections, linkages, and keystones relates to the steeplechase allegory. As Frou-Frou in the horse race, Anna, initially hesitant, soon submits to Vronsky's appeal, rationalizing much of her guilt because of the power and depth of her love for Vronsky. She and Vronsky resolutely confront and for a time largely overcome obstacles placed on their path by society, her forsaken family, and her own gradually increasing disillusionment regarding her relationship with Vronsky. Finally, even Anna and Vronsky's love cools and loses its "zest," and she and Vronsky are tripped up by relatively insignificant obstacles. Again, most important, Anna is unable to abide a man who is not essentially absorbed in her alone. Her chagrin, jealousy, and despair combine with Vronsky's insensitivity, annoyance, and resentment to cause Anna's disaster. Because this all is foreshadowed in the complexly allegorical steeplechase and relates to it throughout the novel, the steeplechase arguably may be considered *the* principal keystone of *Anna Karenina's* architecture or structure. Very significant, this structure shelters and enshrines much of Tolstoy's deepest and most essential message concerning the utter futility of seeking enduring happiness in even the most defensible and sincere adulterous relationship, which must, Tolstoy asserts, finally inflict devastating suffering upon *all* concerned, including both the inevitably disillusioned, guilty perpetrators and, most sadly, the innocent but gravely wounded victims.

SELECT BIBLIOGRAPHY

Adelman, Gary. *Anna Karenina: the Bitterness of Ecstasy.* Boston: Twayne Publishers, 1990.

Alexandrov, Vladimir E. *Limits to Interpretation. The Meanings of* Anna Karenina. Madison: The University of Wisconsin Press, 2004.

Barran, Thomas. "Anna's Dreams" in *Approaches to Teaching Tolstoy's* Anna Karenina. Ed. Liza Knapp and Amy Mandelker. New York: The Modern Language Association of America, 2003:161-65.

Bilinkis, Ia.S. Anna Karenina *L. N. Tolstogo i russkaia literature 1870-kh godov.* Leningrad: Tipografiia No. 5, 1970.

Blackmur, R.P. "*Anna Karenina*: The Dialectic of Incarnation" in Leo Tolstoy. *Anna Karenina.* Norton Critical Edition. Ed. George Gibian. New York: W.W. Norton & Co., 1970:899-917.

Brittan, Simon. *Poetry, Symbol, and Allegory. Interpreting Metaphorical Language from Plato to the Present.* Charlottesville and London: University of Virginia Press, 2003.

Cruise, Edwina J., "The Sources for the Steeplechase in *Anna Karenina*" in *Tolstoy Studies Journal,* vol. 12 (2000):1-8.

Dal', Vladimir. *Tolkovyi slovar' zhivogo velikorusskogo iazyka.* Reprintnoe izdanie v 4-kh tomakh. Sankt-Peterburg: Diamant, 1996.

Eikhenbaum, Boris. *Lev Tolstoi. Semidesiatye gody.* Leningrad: Khudozhestvennaia literature, 1974

Emerson, Caryl. "Prosaics in *Anna Karenina*: Pro and Con" in *Tolstoy Studies Journal,* vol. 8 (1995-96):150-176.

Ermilov, V. *Roman L.N. Tolstogo* Anna Karenina. Moskva: Gosizdat, 1963.

Gustafson, Richard F. *Leo Tolstoy. Resident and Stranger.* Princeton: Princeton University Press, 1986.

Jackson, Robert Louis. "Chance and Design in *Anna Karenina*" in *The Disciplines of Criticism. Essays in Literary Theory, Interpretation, and History.* Ed. Peter Demetz, Thomas Greene, and Lowry Nelson, Jr. New Haven: Yale University Press, 1968:315-29

_____. "The Night Journey: Anna Karenina's Return to Saint Petersburg" in *Approaches to Teaching Tolstoy's* Anna Karenina. Ed Liza Knapp and Amy Mandelker. NY: The Modern Language Association, 2003:150-60.

Jahn, Gary R. "The Image of the Railroad in *Anna Karenina. Slavic and East European Journal,* vol. 25, no. 2 (summer 1981):1-10.

Katz, Michael R. *Dreams and the Unconscious in Nineteenth-Century Russian Fiction.* Hanover: University Press of New England, 1984.

Knapp, Liza. "The Estates of Pokrovskoe and Vosdvizhenskoe: Tolstoy's Labyrinth of Linkings in *Anna Karenina*" in *Tolstoy Studies Journal,* vol. 8 (1995-96):81-98.

Lönnqvist, Barbara. *"Anna Karenina"* in *The Cambridge Companion to Tolstoy.* Ed. Donna Tussing Orwin. Cambridge: Cambridge University Press, 2002:80-95.

Literaturnoe nasledstvo, tom 69, kn. 1-ia. *Lev Tolstoi.* Red. S.A. Makashin. Moskva: Izdatel'stvo Akademii nauk, 1961.

Mandelker Amy. *Framing* Anna Karenina. *Tolstoy, the Woman Question, and the Victorian Novel.* Columbus: Ohio State University Press, 1993.

Merriam-Webster's Encyclopedia of Literature. Ed. Kathleen Kuiper. Springfield, Massachusetts: Merriam-Webster, Inc., 1995.

Morson, Gary Saul. Anna Karenina *in Our Time. Seeing More Wisely.* New Haven: Yale University Press, 2007.

_____. "Anna Karenina's Omens" in *Freedom and Responsibility in Russian Literature.* Ed. Elizabeth Cheresh Allen and Gary Saul Morson. Evanston: Northwestern University Press, 1995:134-52.

_____. "Poetic Justice, False Listening, and Falling in Love: or Why Anna Refuses a Divorce" in *Tolstoy Studies Journal,* vol. 8 (1995-96): 177-197.

Nabokov, Vladimir Vladimirovich. *Lectures on Russian Literature.* Ed. Fredson Bowers. New York: Harcourt Brace Jovanich, 1981.

Orwin, Donna T. *Tolstoy's Art and Thought, 1847-1880.* Ewing, N.J.: Princeton University Press, 1993.

Quinn, Edward. *A Dictionary of Literary and Thematic Terms.* New York: Facts on File, Inc., 1999.

Rice, James. "Some Observations on Stiva's Dream" in *Tolstoy Studies Journal,* vol. 8 (1995-96):117-124.

Roundtable Discussion: "Amy Mandelker's *Framing* Anna Karenina: *Tolstoy, the Woman Question, and the Victorian Novel"* in *Tolstoy Studies Journal,* vol. 8 (1995-96):129-37.

Schultze, Sydney. *The Structure of* Anna Karenina. Ann Arbor, Michigan: Ardis, 1982.

Tindall, William York. *The Literary Symbol.* New York: Columbia U. Press, 1955.

Tolstoi, L.N. *Polnoe sobranie sochinenii.* Red. V.G. Chertkov. Moskva: Gosizdat Khudozhestvennaia literatura, t. 20, 1939.

Tolstoi, L.N. *Sobranie sochinenii v dvadtsati tomakh.* Red. N.N. Akopova. Moskva: Khudozhestvennaia literatura, tt. 8-9, 1963.

Tolstoy, Leo. *Anna Karenina. A Novel in Eight Parts.* Transl. Richard Pevear and Larissa Volokhonsky. New York: Viking Press, 2001.

Tolstoy, Leo. *What is Art? And Essays on Art.* Trans. Alymer Maude. London: Oxford U. Press, 1962.

Turner, C.J.G. *A Karenina Companion.* Waterloo, Ontario, Canada: Wilfrid Laurier University Press, 1993.

Wasiolek, Edward. *Tolstoy's Major Fiction.* Chicago: The University of Chicago Press, 1978.

Weir, Justin. "Anna Incommunicada: Language and Consciousness in *Anna Karenina*" in *Tolstoy Studies Journal*, vol. 8 (1995-96):99-11.

Zhdanov, V.A. "K istorii sozdaniia *Anny Kareninoi*" in *Literaturnoe nasledstvo*, t. 69, kn.1-ia. *Lev Tolstoi*. Red. S.A. Makashin. Moskva: Izd-vo Akademii nauk, 1961:307-442.

_____, sost. *Opisanie rukopisei khudozhestvennykh proizvedenii L.N. Tolstogo*. Moskva: Izd-vo Akademii nauk, 1955.

_____. *Tvorcheskaia istoriia* Anny Kareninoi. *Materialy i Nabliudeniia*. Moskva: Sovetskii pisatel', 1957.

INDEX

Adelman, Gary	41n4
Alexandrov, Vladimir	21n4
Allegory,	
Diana and Kuzovlev	
as Betsy and Tushkevich	66-67
Allegory,	
Frou-Frou as Anna	60-61
Allegory,	
Gladiator as Karenin	62-64
Allegory,	
Makhotin as Seryozha	64-66
Allegory and symbol, definitions	13-14
Blackmur, R.P.	18
Brittan, Simon	13
Cruise, Edwina J.	61n2, 105n2
Dal', Vladimir	43
"Death of Ivan Ilych"	47
Drafts of *Anna Karenina*,	
the first draft	104-111
Drafts of *Anna Karenina*,	
the second draft	111-113

Dream, Anna's of her two husbands   48, 50-53
Dream, Anna's of the muzhik   37, 44-58
Dream, Vronsky's of the muzhik   36, 43-44

Eikhenbaum, Boris   13, 61
Emerson, Caryl   12n1, 58n9
Encyclopedia of Literature   14

Fet, Afanasii   13
Frou-Frou, origin of   61

Goethe   13
Gustafson, Richard   12n1, 20n3, 34-35 37n2

Hadji Murat   12
"How Much Land Does a Man Need?"   15

Jackson, Robert L.   26n1, 29
Jahn, Gary   28-29
Jubilee Edition   111n3

Knapp, Liza   12n1, 20n2

Labyrinth of linkages, Tolstoy's usage   18, 115-16
Lönnqvist, Barbara   20n2, 45n6

Mandelker, Amy   12n1
Meihac, Henri and Ludovic Halevy   61
Miliutin, A.D.   105n2
Moral message, Tolstoy's   99-100, 118
Morson, Gary Saul   56n8, 92n2

Nabokov, Vladimir   70n1

Index

Orwin, Donna T.	12n1
Principle of reasonable probability, definition	16
Principle of reasonable probability, six motifs: coincidental or intentional	99
Principle of reasonable probability, steeplechase's named participants	61, 66
Rachinskii, S.A.	19
Resurrection	100
Rice, James	12n1
Schopenhauer, Arthur	13, 42n1
Strakhov, Nikolai	17-18, 19
Structure of *Anna Karenina*, sequences and episodes	70-72
Structure of *Anna Karenina*, sequences and the six motifs	77-99
Structure of *Anna Karenina*, six motifs	72-77, 118
Symbol, the cold post	25, 27-29
Symbol, the knife	29-32
Symbol, the muzhik (Russian peasant)	34-58, 116-17
Symbol, the storm	25-27
Symbol, the torn-off sheet of iron	55, 117

Symbol and allegory,
    the two clusters   21-22

"Three Deaths"   17
"Three Hermits, The"   15
Tindall, William York   14
Tiutchev, Fedor   13
Turner, C.J.G.   42n5

War and Peace   12, 20
Wasiolek, Edward   11, 30n2, 35, 56
Weaknesses, Anna's   22, 58
Weaknesses, Vronsky's   22, 60, 68
Weir, Justin   12n1

Zhdanov, V.A.   104n1, 112n3

www.ingramcontent.com/pod-product-compliance
Lightning Source LLC
Chambersburg PA
CBHW070547090426
42735CB00013B/3097